COOL GROOVY AND FAB!

QUOTES FROM THE SWINGING '60s

DAVE RICHARDSON

" People in life
quote as they
please, so we have
the right to quote
as we please.
Therefore I show
people quoting,
merely making sure
that they quote what
pleases me "

JEAN-LUC GODARD

ART DIRECTION Dave Richardson   DESIGN Julia Kennedy
Special thanks to John Parkin   Front cover photo courtesy of MIRRORPIX
Copyright ©Dave Richardson/Perennial Music/PlayDigital 2019

"If you remember the Sixties, you really weren't there"

CHARLES FLEISCHER

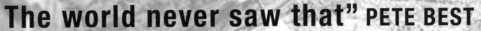
"We were at our best when we were playing the dance halls of Liverpool and Hamburg The world never saw that" PETE BEST

THE SENSATIONAL SIXTIES

I'M A BEATLES FAN

LOVE! LOVE! LOVE!

THE SILVER BEATLES

PETE BEST
GEORGE HARRISON

JOHN LENNON
PAUL McCARTNEY

APPEARING AT THE

CAVERN CLUB
LIVERPOOL

JAN. 4 THRU 18 - 1962

"I'm happier than I would have been with the Beatles"
PETE BEST

"We don't like their sound. Groups of guitars are on the way out" DECCA EXECUTIVE, 1962 – after turning the Beatles down!

We're more popular than Jesus now
JOHN LENNON

"There's no outdoing the Beatles"
BRIAN WILSON

None of us wanted to be the bass player. In our minds he was the fat guy who always played at the back
PAUL McCARTNEY

We got £25 a week in the early Sixties when we were first with Brian Epstein, when we played the clubs GEORGE HARRISON

We thought that if we lasted for two to three years that would be fantastic RINGO STARR

"The Beatles were in a different stratosphere, a different planet to the rest of us. All I know is when I heard 'Love Me Do' on the radio, I remember walking down the street and knowing my life was going to be completely different now the Beatles were in it" JUSTIN HAYWARD

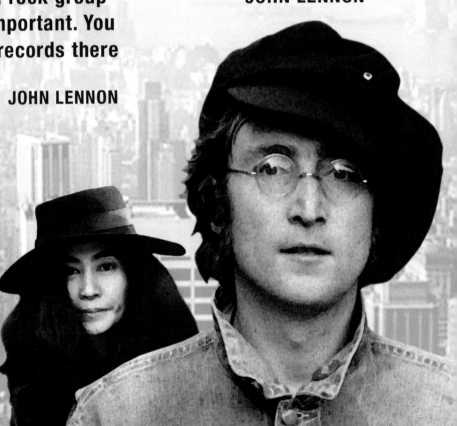

"Life is what happens when you are busy making other plans"

"Music is everybody's possession. It's only publishers who think that people own it"

"As usual, there is a great woman behind every idiot"

"It's just natural, it's not a great disaster. People keep talking about it like it's The End of The Earth. It's only a rock group that split up, it's nothing important. You know, you have all the old records there if you want to reminisce"

JOHN LENNON

"If there's such a thing as genius, I am one. And if there isn't, I don't care"

JOHN LENNON

"I did not break up the Beatles. You can't have it both ways. If you're going to blame me for breaking the Beatles up, you should be thankful that I made them into myth rather than a crumbling group"

YOKO ONO

"All the truth in the world adds up to one big lie" BOB DYLAN

WHERE HAVE ALL THE FLOWERS GONE

"The only thing that's been a worse flop than the organization of non-violence has been the organization of violence" JOAN BAEZ

"NO ONE IS FREE, EVEN THE BIRDS

"I would say that I'm a nonviolent soldier. In place of weapons of violence, you have to use your mind, your heart, your sense of humor, every faculty available to you … because no one has the right to take the life of another human being" JOAN BAEZ

"Anything I can sing, I call a song. Anything I can't sing I call a poem. Anything I can't sing or anything that's too long to be a poem, I call a novel" BOB DYLAN

ARE CHAINED TO THE SKY" BOB DYLAN

"I became interested in folk music because I had to make it somehow"

"I define nothing. Not beauty, not patriotism. I take each thing as it is, without prior rules about what it should be"

"I'll let you be in my dreams if I can be in yours"

"There is nothing so stable as change"

"Well, the future for me is already a thing of the past"

"You can't do something forever"

"All I can do is be me – whoever that is"

"Chaos is a friend of mine. It's like I accept him, does he accept me?"

BOB DYLAN

> " I'm speaking for all of us. I'm the spokesman for a generation "

BOB DYLAN

DONT LOOK BACK

US 61 ★ BOB DYLAN ★ BOB DYLAN ★ BOB DYLAN ★ BOB DYLAN ★

"Having a place in this society is a society in which one would

"On one level the Sixties revolt was an impressive illustration of Lenin's remark that the capitalist will sell you the rope to hang him with" ELLEN WILLIS

"Marches alone won't bring integration when human respect is disintegratin'" BARRY McGUIRE

"All power to the people!" BOBBY SEALE

"The first duty of a revolutionary is to get away with it" ABBIE HOFFMAN

"Our smiles are political banners and our nakedness is our picket sign!" JERRY RUBIN

"You can't separate peace from freedom because no one can be at peace unless he has his freedom" MALCOLM X

far less important than creating want to have a place" MARIO SAVIO

"Clearly this notion of violent, total youth revolution and takeover is an idea whose time has come – which speaks not well for the idea, but ill for the time" LESTER BANGS

"The only way to support a revolution is to make your own" ABBIE HOFFMAN

"I see America through the eyes of a victim. I don't see the American dream, I see an American nightmare"
MALCOM X

"The first resistance to social change is to say it's not necessary" GLORIA STEINEM

POWER TO THE PEOPLE

WE SHALL NOT BE MOVED

BE FAMOUS FOR FIFTEEN MINUTES"

ANDY WARHOL

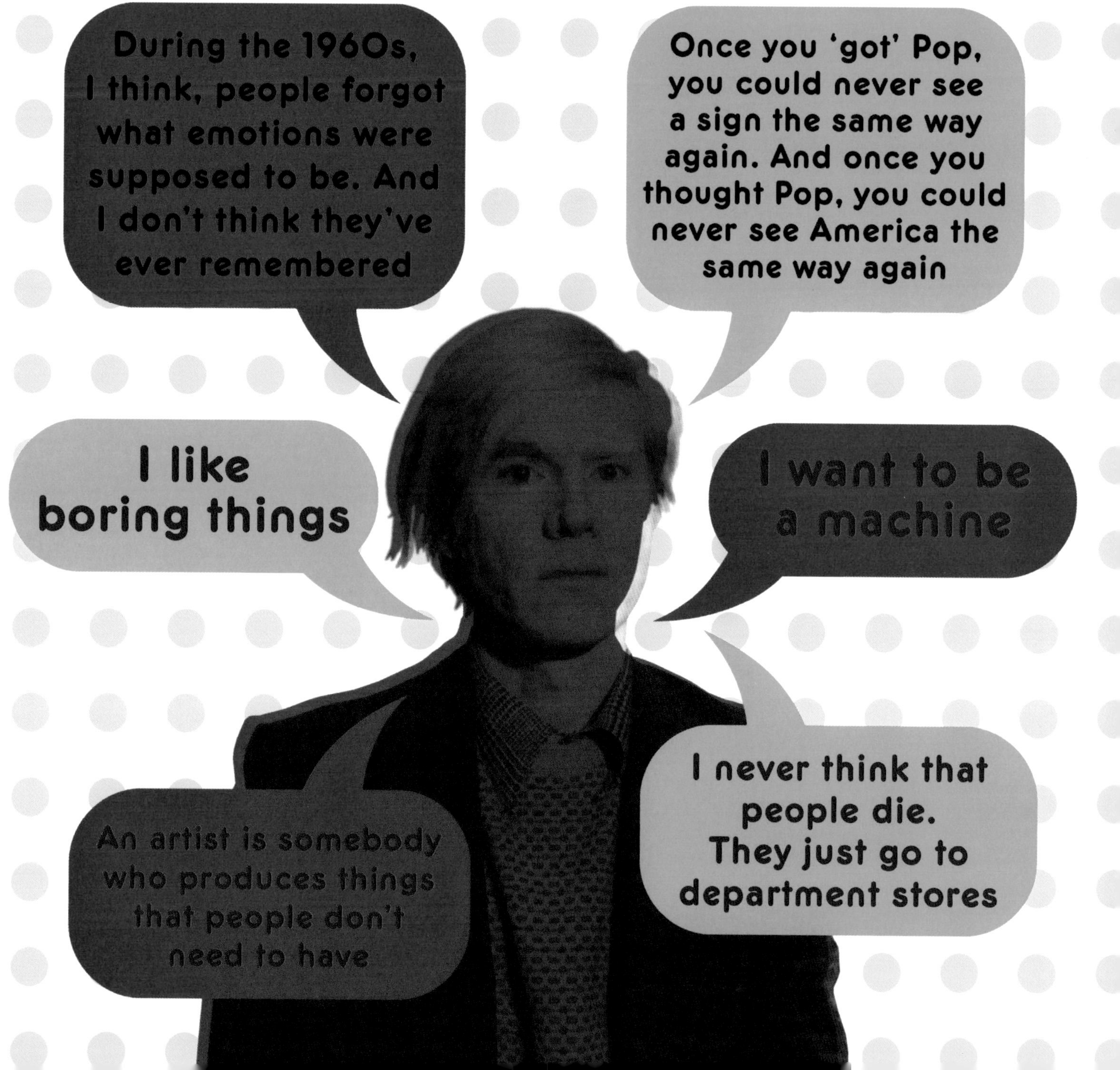

"I COMPARE THE TWIST TO THE ELECTRIC LIGHT, THE TWIST IS ME, AND I'M IT. I'M THE ELECTRIC LIGHT"
CHUBBY CHECKER

"GOT A NEW DANCE AND IT GOES LIKE THIS THE NAME OF THIS DANCE IS THE PEPPERMINT TWIST"
JOEY DEE & THE STARLITERS

"COME ON LET'S TWIST AGAIN LIKE YOU DID LAST SUMMER
YEAH, LET'S TWIST AGAIN LIKE YOU DID LAST YEAR"
CHUBBY CHECKER

"WATUSI IS THE
DANCE TO DO
WAH-A, WAH,
WAH-A WATUSI
SEE'MON AND
TAKE A CHANCE
AND GET-A WITH
THIS DANCE
WAH, WAH-A WATUSI
OH, BABY, IT'S THE
DANCE MADE-A
FOR ROMANCE"
THE ORLONS

"EVERYBODY'S DOING A
BRAND-NEW DANCE,
NOW (COME ON BABY,
DO THE LOCO-MOTION)
I KNOW YOU'LL GET TO
LIKE IT IF YOU GIVE IT A
CHANCE, NOW (COME ON BABY,
DO THE LOCO-MOTION)
MY LITTLE BABY SISTER CAN DO IT WITH ME
IT'S EASIER THAN LEARNING YOUR A-B-C'S
SO COME ON, COME ON, DO THE
LOCO-MOTION WITH ME" LITTLE EVA

"Float like a butterfly, sting like a bee"

MUHAMMAD ALI

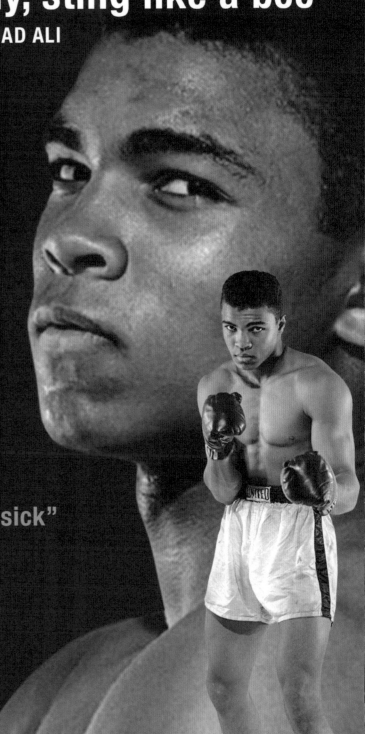

"I've wrestled with alligators.
I've tussled with a whale.
I done handcuffed lightning.
And throw thunder in jail"

"I am the greatest, I said that
even before I knew I was"

"I'm young; I'm handsome;
I'm fast. I can't possibly
be beat"

"I'm so mean, I make medicine sick"

"If you even dream of beating
me you'd better wake up
and apologize"

"I DESIGNED THE MINISKIRT THAT CAUSED SO MUCH HAVOC IN THE SIXTIES" MARY QUANT

"Most of my memories of the Sixties are ones of optimism, high spirits and confidence"

"Of course, I remember when everybody was thin. It wasn't until I went to America in the Sixties that I saw anyone who wasn't skinny thin"

"As well as being a creative genius, Vidal Sassoon was a formative figure of the Sixties. Along with the pill and the miniskirt, his influence was truly liberating"

"Hairdressers are a wonderful breed. You work one-on-one with another human being and the object is to make them feel so much better and to look at themselves with a twinkle in their eye" VIDAL SASSOON

"Good taste is death. Vulgarity is life"

"ENGLAND SWINGS LIKE

BIBA

"I've got BIBA flowing through my veins"
BARBARA HULANICKI

I WAS LORD KITCHENER'S VALET

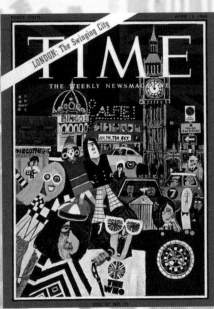

LONDON: The Swinging City
TIME
THE WEEKLY NEWSMAGAZINE

BIBA

"There was nothing in between baby clothes and adult clothes until BIBA came along in 1963"
MOLLIE PARKIN

"Everywhere the Carnabetian army marches on" RAY DAVIES

A PENDULUM DO" ROGER MILLER

"In the '60s it was all about the legs"
BARBARA HULANICKI

"She tried to make the swinging
city scene and now there's not
a place that Polly hasn't been"
RAY DAVIES

"London is the
most swinging
city in the world
at the moment"

DIANA VREELAND, Vogue

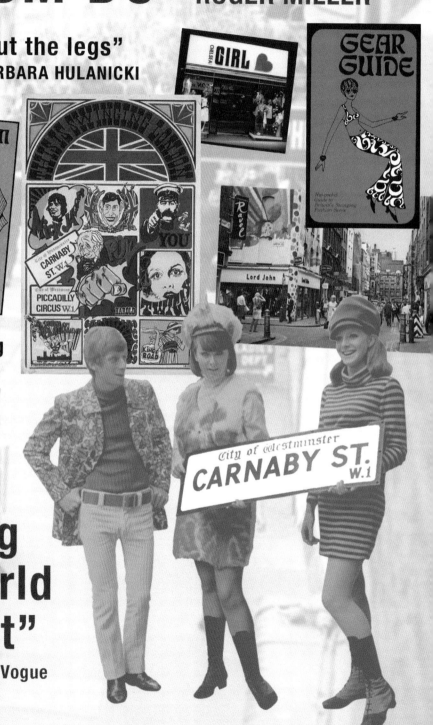

"MEIN FUHRER! I CAN WALK!"
DR STRANGELOVE

"GENTLEMEN! YOU CAN'T FIGHT IN HERE! THIS IS THE WAR ROOM" PRESIDENT MERKIN MUFFLEY

"Thankfully I'm not endlessly ambitious, but I have done some crazy ambitious things like buying an island off the west coast of Scotland in the late Sixties"
JACK BRUCE

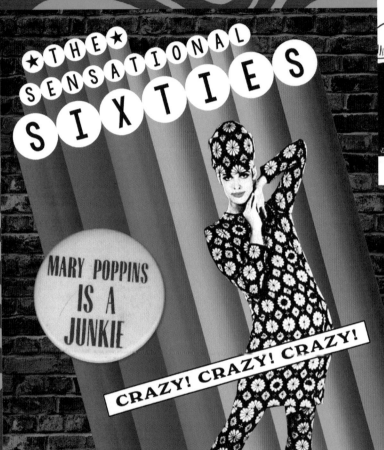

Peter Sellers · George C. Scott
in Stanley Kubrick's
Dr. Strangelove
Or:
How
I Learned
To
Stop
Worrying
And
Love
The
Bomb
the hot-line suspense comedy

also starring Sterling Hayden · Keenan Wynn · Slim Pickens and introducing Tracy Reed...
Screenplay by Stanley Kubrick, Peter George & Terry Southern Based on the book "Red Alert" by Peter George
Produced & Directed by Stanley Kubrick · A Columbia Pictures Release

"YOU HAVE TO GO ON AND BE CRAZY. CRAZINESS IS LIKE HEAVEN"
JIMI HENDRIX

"YOU KNOW, A LONG TIME AGO BEING CRAZY MEANT SOMETHING. NOWADAYS EVERYBODY'S CRAZY"
CHARLES MANSON

"All the leaves are brown (all the leaves are brown)
And the sky is grey (and the sky is grey)"
THE MAMAS AND THE PAPAS

"I know when 'California Dreamin' was first released, we heard it on KFWB or KHJ or something, and it was so exciting to hear the record come on the radio"
MICHELLE PHILLIPS

"One of my biggest likes is 'going very fast backwards' and what I really don't like is 'going very slow forwards'" DENNY DOHERTY

"Everybody used to think that John Phillips, who wrote the songs, was also the main voice of the group, but it wasn't – it was the angelic voice of Denny Doherty. He was often overlooked but it was really his voice that carried the group"
LARRY LEBLANC, Billboard

"My role in the Mamas and Papas was basically just to sing"
CASS ELLIOT

"I don't like out of tune people and being late for rehearsals"
JOHN PHILLIPS

"Sex is more exciting on the screen and between

"I never miss a chance to have sex or appear on television" GORE VIDAL

"There is nothing safe about sex. There never will be" NORMAN MAILER

LET THERE BE LOVE

MAKE LOVE NOT WAR

THE LOVE TRIBE

Freak out, love in, do your thing the way it is in the East Village

a novel by Joseph Mathewson

LOVE

"Fantasy love is much better than reality love" ANDY WARHOL

"I have tried sex with both men and women. I found I liked it"
DUSTY SPRINGFIELD

the pages than between the sheets" ANDY WARHOL

"I love you. I love you. I tell you. Now walk on me. Spit on me.
Stomp on my face" PROF. HENRI – BELLE DE JOUR

"I'm lost.
I can't help
it. I can't
fight it.
I know
I'll have to
atone for
everything
one day"
SÉVERINE

"Benjamin,
would
you
like
me to
seduce
you?"
MRS
ROBINSON

"First
we'll
have
an orgy.
Then
we'll
go see
Tony
Bennett"
TED
HENDERSON

"Make love ... You don't even
know my psychocardiogram!"
BARBARELLA

A GAS - having a fun time
ALL SHOW AND NO GO - looks good superficially
APE - crazy or mad
BAD - awesome
BADASS - trouble maker
BEAN WAGON - cheap restaurant, or a lowered car driven by Mexican Americans
BEAT FEET - leave quickly
BENCH RACING - sitting around and talking about the speed of their cars
BLAST - a good time, a loud party
BLITZED - drunk
BOGART - to keep for yourself, to bully
BONE YARD - a place to put junk or wrecked cars
BOOB TUBE - television
BOOGIE BOARD - a short surfboard
BOOKIN' - going fast in a car
BOSS - fantastic
BREW - beer
BRODY - skid half a circle in a car with the brakes locked
BUG - to bother
BUG OUT - to leave
BUMMER - a bad thing or unpleasant experience
BURN RUBBER - squeal tires and leave rubber on the road
CATCH SOME RAYS - get out in the sun
CHERRY - mint condition
CHICKEN/PLAY CHICKEN - two cars driving towards each other

CHINESE FIREDRILL - when four people get out of a car at a right light and exchange places in the car
CHOP - to cut someone down verbally
CHROME DOME - bald man
COOL HEAD - nice guy
CRASH - sleep
CUT OUT - leave the area quickly

'60s SLANG

DECKED OUT - dressed up
DEUCE - putting two fingers up in a peace symbol
DIBS - ownership
DIG - understand
DON'T FLIP YOUR WIG - don't be upset
DOVE - a peace lover
DOWNER - an unpleasant experience

DRAG - someone or something that is boring
DROPOUT - refuse to conform with society
FAB - fabulous
FAB FOUR - The Beatles
FAR OUT - awesome
FINK - tattletale
FIVE FINGER DISCOUNT - stolen
FLAKE - useless person
FLAKE OFF - leave
FLIP FLOPS - thongs
FLOWER POWER - the peaceful protest movement of the 60s counterculture
FOX - good looking woman
FREAK OUT - get excited and lose control
FREEDOM RIDERS - civil rights protesters
GIMME SOME SKIN - to ask someone to slap or shake your hand in agreement
GONE - under the influence of drugs
GNARLY - difficult or big
GROOVY - outstanding or nice
GROADY - dirty
GRUNGY - looking shabby or dirty
HACKED - made someone mad
HAIRY - difficult or out of control
HANG LOOSE - take it very easy
HANG TOUGH - to stick with something difficult
HAWK - a supporter of war
HEAVY - a serious or intense subject

HIPPIE/HIPPY - a member of the counterculture; a free sprited, unconventional person

HOG - to take over so that someone else cannot use

HOT DOG - show-off

HUNK - good looking guy

IN THE GROOVE - a person who is part of the in-crowd

JAM - play music together

JAZZED - excited

JELLY ROLL - heroin

KICKS - something done for pleasure

KISS OFF - dismiss

KISS UP - someone who will do anything to gain favor by another person

KNOCKED UP - pregnant

LAID BACK - relaxed

LAY IT ON ME - tell me

LAY RUBBER - stop fast and leave wheel marks on the road

MAKE OUT - kissing

MIDNIGHT AUTO SUPPLY - stolen auto parts

MIRROR WARMER - woman who spends a lot of time looking in the mirror

MOON - to drop your pants

MOP-TOP - someone with a Beatle-style haircut

NEATO - awesome

NIFTY - stylish or very good

NO SWEAT - No problem

OLD LADY - girlfriend/wife, sometimes mother

OLD MAN - boyfriend/husband, sometimes father

ON THE MAKE - looking for a date

OUTTA SIGHT - awesome

PAD - where you sleep or live

PANTY WAIST - a boy who does not have a tough personality

PASSION PIT - drive-in movie

PEEL OUT - accelerate quickly, leaving rubber on the road

PEGGERS - jeans with tight calfs and ankles

PIG - police officer

PIG OUT - overeat

PORT HOLER - a sailor on a ship

POUND - to beat someone up

RACE FOR PINKS - race cars when the winner keeps the loser's car

RIGHT ON - OK, a term of agreement

RIP OFF - steal

SCARF - eat fast

SCORE - go all the way with a girl

SCRATCH - money

SHADES - sunglasses

SHOT DOWN - rejected

SHOTGUN - passenger seat

SKAG OR SKANK - an ugly girl

SKIRT - a girl

SKUZZ/SKUZZ BUCKET - disgusting person or thing

SLUG BUG - Volkswagen Beetle

SOCK IT TO ME - Let me have it

SOLID - I understand

SOUPED UP - lots of extra equipment

SPLIT - to leave

SPONGE - live off of someone else's money or belongings

SQUARE - someone who is not cool

STOKED - likes someone or something a lot

STONED - high on pot

STUCK UP - conceited

SWEAT HOG - fat girl or boy

TENNIES - tennis shoes

THE MAN - any authority figure who maintained the corporate, legal and political status quo

THREADS - clothes

TICKED OFF - angry

TIGHT - very friendly

TOKE - a puff from a marijuana cigarette

TOOLING - driving around

TOUGH - great looking

TUFF - cool or very enjoyable

TUNE OUT - ignore

TURN OFF - to respulse someone

TRUCKIN' - moving quickly

TWICE PIPES - two muffler tail pipes

TWITCHIN' - great or awesome

UNGLUED - upset

UNREAL - so outstanding that it was difficult to believe

UPTIGHT - tense and unable to enjoy life

WAY OUT - beyond explanation

WHAT'S YOUR BAG, MAN? - what are you into? what's your problem?

WIPE OUT - to fail in a big way or to fall off the surfboard

ZILCH - zero

ZIT - pimple

"It's not what you'd call

PLAY IT COOL

seventeen

TWIGGY
models a wardrobe
designed by
seventeen

You can STILL
make money
this summer

SUMMER
BEAUTY
LIFESAVERS

SEX:
a student report

VOGUE

FASHION
FORECAST
YOUR NEXT
BEST LOOKS

THE
BEAUTIFUL
PEOPLE:
THEIR
HAIR AND
MAKEUP THIS
SUMMER

OUT
DAMNED
SPOT!

FORGET
OXFAM
FEED TWIGGY

a figure, is it?" TWIGGY

"From as far back as I can remember, I was always insecure about my looks, whether it was my flat chest, my skinny legs, or how to cope with my body as it changed. With hindsight, I can see I was different. I was given a body that worked for photographic modelling and a photogenic face"

"There's no need to dress like everyone else. It's much more fun to create your own look"

"For special occasions, I love pretty dresses, but nothing too frou-frou!"

"I hate being nostalgic about the Sixties"
DAVID BAILEY

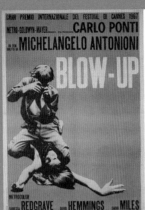  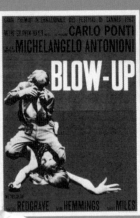

"The Sixties was a time of breaking down class barriers, although I think class still exists today in some areas"
DAVID BAILEY

"I never liked being photo-graphed. I just happened to be good at it"

"If you take off the makeup, I'm ugly"
JEAN SHRIMPTON

"Being handsome wasn't much of a burden. It worked for me"

"I've been used by women all my life. Fortunately"
DAVID BAILEY

"It is still a puzzle to me that I ever became a model. I am an extremely private person and I do not have the temperament for fame. I think I was rather ashamed of this trivial way of earning a living" JEAN SHRIMPTON

"We really were vicious. In the beginning if anyone was the slightest bit flaky in a recording session, they were really in for a hard time. When you're young you put the knife in" MICK JAGGER

"Brian should have been put in a straitjacket and treated. I used to know Brian quite well. The Stones have always been a group I really dug. Dug all the dodgy aspects of them as well, and Brian Jones has always been what I've regarded as one of the dodgy aspects. The way he fitted in and the way he didn't was one of the strong dynamics of the group. When he stopped playing with them, I thought that dynamic was going to be missing, but it still seems to be there. Perhaps the fact that he's dead has made that dynamic kind of permanent. A little bit of love might have sorted him out. I don't think his death was necessarily a bad thing for Brian. I think he'll do better next time. I believe in reincarnation" PETE TOWNSHEND, on his tribute song 'A Normal Day For Brian'

"When people talk about the '60s, I never think that was me there. It was me and I was in it, but I was never enamored with all that. It's supposed to be sex and drugs and rock and roll and I'm not really like that. I've never really seen the Rolling Stones as anything" CHARLIE WATTS

"I've never had a problem with drugs. I've had problems with the police"

"About myself I have no great illusions. I know what I am. I know what I'm good at. I know what I ain't. I'm always hoping to surprise myself"

KEITH RICHARDS

"My first record I owned was by Les Paul"

"I'm always shy in front of an audience, so I'm always at the back, in the shadows, just doing it. I don't like the front, the adulation"

BILL WYMAN

SPECIAL SPECIAL SPECIAL
Here's what you've been waiting for
the NEW
ROLLING STONES
single it's all over now F11R84
Rush released - rush to get it DE

THE ROLLING STONES

"We belong to a generation that's separate from any other. We believe in what we're doing. We're happy to have the kids screaming for us. It gets me down to think that a lot of them will one day disappear into the drab nest. I hope all of them won't. If only the whole world could stay young" MICK JAGGER

"HITCHCOCK NEVER LOOKED THROUGH THE VIEWFINDER BECAUSE HE HAD EVERY FRAME OF THE MOVIE IN HIS HEAD FROM THE FIRST DAY OF SHOOTING" SEAN CONNERY

"The more successful the villain, the more successful the picture"

"Blondes make the best victims. They're like virgin snow that shows up the bloody footprints"

"The length of a film should be directly related to the endurance of the human bladder"

"For me, the cinema is not a slice of life, but a piece of cake"

"The only way to get rid of my fears is to make films about them"

"Give them pleasure; the same pleasure they have when they wake up from a nightmare"

"What is drama but life with the dull bits cut out"

"Logic is dull"

"I'm frightened of my own movies"

"A good film is when the price of the dinner, the theatre admission and the babysitter were worth it"

"Self-plagiarism is style"

"In feature films the director is God; in documentary films God is the director"

"If you can't do it naturally, then fake it"

"I NEVER SAID ACTORS ARE CATTLE; WHAT I SAID WAS ALL ACTORS SHOULD BE TREATED LIKE CATTLE" ALFRED HITCHCOCK

"A boy's best friend is his mother" NORMAN BATES, Psycho

"I hardly think a few birds are going to bring about the end of the world"
MRS BUNDY, The Birds

"Against all the evidence, Michael, I'd say you had a very unscientific mind"
SARA SHERMAN, Torn Curtain

"Hitch was not only my director, he was my drama coach, which was fantastic"
TIPPI HENDREN, Marnie

"I've been shot ... just a little" FRANÇOIS PICARD, Topaz

"FASTER, FASTER, FASTER, UNTIL THE THRILL

"Is she really going out
with him?"
"Well, there she is.
Let's ask her"
"Betty, is that Jimmy's
ring you're wearing?"
"Mm-hm"
"Gee, it must be great
riding with him"
"Is he picking you up
after school today?"
"Mm-mm"
"By the way, where
did you meet him?"
"I met him at the
candy store.
He turned around
and smiled at me.
You get the picture?"
"Yes, we see"
"That's when I fell for
the leader of the pack"
THE SHANGRI-LAS

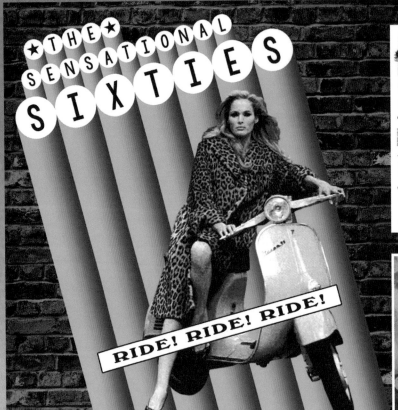

★ THE ★ SENSATIONAL SIXTIES

RIDE! RIDE! RIDE!

"He rode into the night, accelerated his motorbike
I cried to him in fright, don't do it, don't do it, don't do it
He said to me you are the one I want to be with
He said to me you are the one who my love I shall give
One day he'll know how hard I prayed for him to live
Please wait at the gate of heaven for me, Terry"
TWINKLE

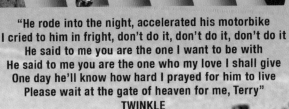

"Rebellion is the only thing that keeps you alive"
REBECCA, Girl On A Motorcycle

OF SPEED OVERCOMES THE FEAR OF DEATH"
HUNTER S THOMPSON

"Easy Rider was never a motorcycle movie to me. A lot of it was about politically what was going on in the country"
DENNIS HOPPER

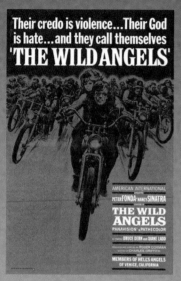

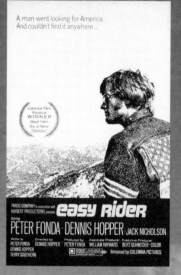

"WE WANNA BE FREE!
We wanna be free to do what we wanna do.
We wanna be free to ride. We wanna be free to ride our machines without being hassled by The Man! ... And we wanna get loaded.
And we wanna have a good time. And that's what we are gonna do.
We are gonna have a good time ...
WE ARE GONNA HAVE A PARTY!"
PETER FONDA, The Wild Angels

"Henry Fonda's son. That's how everybody identified me until Easy Rider came along. Good old Captain America" PETER FONDA

"Teens identify with my lyrics, they were going through the very same things I was singing about"
HELEN SHAPIRO

GROOVY CHICKS AND HOT HITS!

"I love my feet"
SANDIE SHAW

"In the '60s we didn't choose our own songs, we were told by the record company what we had to sing"
SUSAN MAUGHAN

"My story is really an affirmation of my strength and my luck. To live with a great artist like Mick Jagger is a very, very destructive role for a woman trying to be herself. In fact, it can't be done"
MARIANNE FAITHFULL

"I used so much hairspray that I feel personally responsible for global warming"
DUSTY SPRINGFIELD

"There are definitely people who are stuck in the '60s and there are definitely people who think I am and it's just not true" PETULA CLARK

"Back when I was helping put the swing into the swinging '60s, I used to hang out with Cathy McGowan. We'd be doing READY STEADY GO! on TV, and Biba used to make our dresses. We'd be in the flat in Cromwell Road on Friday night, just before the live show, and they'd still be sewing" CILLA BLACK

"I didn't like any British music before The Beatles. For me, it was all about black American music. But then I became a successful pop singer, even though the kind of music I liked was more elitist, which is what I'm trying to get back to" LULU

"A real Mod does not choose to be a Mod, they discover that they are a Mod. It is not just a fashion statement; it is the way you feel and act and express yourself. Mod is in the soul" UNKNOWN

IT'S A MOD MOD WORLD

"The scooter-riding, all-night-dancing instigators of what became, from it's myriad sources, a very British phenomenon. Mod began life as the quint-essential working-class movement of a newly affluent nation – a uniquely British amalgam of American music and European fashions that mixed modern jazz with modernist design in an attempt to escape the drab conformity, snobbery and prudery of life in 1950s Britain. But what started as a popular cult became a mainstream culture, and a style became a revolution" RICHARD WEIGHT

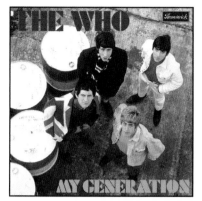

"People try to put us down
(Talkin' 'bout my generation)
Just because we get around
(Talkin' 'bout my generation)
Things they do look awful c-c-cold
(Talkin' 'bout my generation)
Hope I die before I get old"

GO MOD

The Who

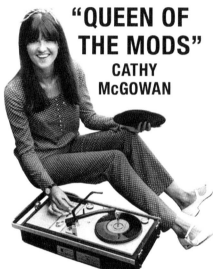

"QUEEN OF
THE MODS"
CATHY
McGOWAN

"I think it's quite
subversive for kids
who haven't got a
lot of money to dress
up in a suit and look
twice as good as
someone who's got
three times as much
money. It's a social
comment" IAN PAGE

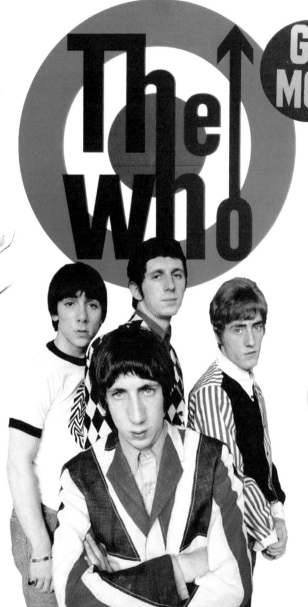

"It was kinda half-baked.
The concept should have run all
the way through. I dunno what
happened there" IAN McLAGAN

GOT MY MOJO WORKING

HOME OF THE BLUES
THE CHECKERBOARD LOUNGE
423 E. 43RD STREET • CHICAGO, ILLINOIS
In Person • Blues Legend
MUDDY WATERS
Lefty Dizz
JUNIOR WELLS & BUDDY GUY
THE ROLLING STONES
12 AM UNTIL • ADMISSION $2
★ SUNDAY NOVEMBER 22

PAUL BUTTERFIELD
AND THE QUICK-SILVER MESSENGER SERVICE
BLUES BAND
9.00 P.M.
FRI.SAT.SUN.
MARCH
25.26.27
FILLMORE AUDITORIUM

MISSISSIPPI FRED McDOWELL
—IN CONCERT.
SAT. 8TH MAR. 1969
AT THE MAYFAIR THEATRE
STRATTON ST. LONDON. W.I. 6PM & 8·30PM
SUPPORTING BILL:-
ALEXIS KORNER
JO-ANN KELLY
IAN ANDERSON'S COUNTRY BLUES BAND.
M.C. MIKE RAVEN
TICKETS 14/- 17/-

r&b at the ricky-tick club
PLAZA BALLROOM, GUILDFORD
10th JAN: **THE ANIMALS**
17th JAN: FROM CHICAGO....
SONNY-BOY WILLIAMSON
WITH **THE YARDBIRDS**
FRIDAYS 8 PM.

"If it wasn't for the British musicians, a lot of us black musicians in America would still be catchin' the hell that we caught long before. So thanks to them, thanks to all you guys. You opened doors that I don't think would have been opened in my lifetime. When white America started paying attention to the Blues, it started opening a lot of doors that had been closed to us" BB KING

LIKE A RELIGION, REALLY" PETER GREEN

"It's an often asked question, 'Why did all these spotty white English boys suddenly start playing Blues in the '60s?' It was recognized as this kind of vibrant music and when I first started playing in a Blues band I just wanted to bring it to a wider public who hadn't really heard it" STEVE WINWOOD

"If you don't know the Blues, there's no point in picking up the guitar and playing rock and roll or any other form of popular music" KEITH RICHARDS

"The basis of everything that I plugged into when I was younger was Blues, and it always stayed with me" ERIC BURDON

"The British feel of Blues has been hard, rather than emotional. Too much emphasis on 12 bar, too little attention to words, far too little originality" ALEXIS KORNER

"The Blues scene now is international. In the '50s it was purely something that you would hear in black clubs, played by black musicians, especially in America. But from the '60s onwards it changed" MICK TAYLOR

"When all the original Blues guys are gone, you start to realize that someone has to tend to the tradition. I recognize that I have some responsibility to keep the music alive, and it's a pretty honorable position to be in" ERIC CLAPTON

"THE BRITISH INVASION. FROM THE BEATLES TO

"Aside from what they did musically, the Beatles were great ambassadors. They made everything English very cool at the time. By the time we got (to America), everyone was ready for us. Just the fact that we were English opened every door for us" PETER NOONE, HERMAN'S HERMITS

"Touring in the 1960s – that was the ultimate high – you feel like the pied piper, or a conductor, knowing how to take an audience up or down. You were champions of the world for that one or two hours of the day" DAVE CLARK

COOL BRITS AND ALL THE HITS!

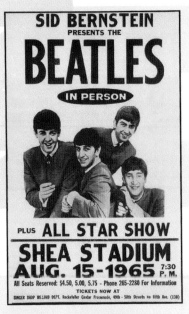

"Oh, Dad's gone down the dogtrack, Mother's playin' bingo
Grannie's boozin' in the parlour, hic, you oughta see the gin go
No one seems to notice me, isn't it a sin
What a crazy world we're livin' in" JOE BROWN

"It was felt that I'd done as much as I could in England. I didn't know what direction I could go, apart from across the sea" DUSTY SPRINGFIELD

"In many respects, being blacklisted by the American Federation of Musicians took away the best years of The Kinks' career when the original band was performing at it's peak"
RAY DAVIES

THE STONES, THE SIXTIES BELONGED TO BRITAIN"

ROLLING STONE MAGAZINE

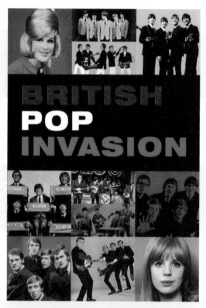

"Most White Americans only discovered the blues with the British invasion" ERIC BURDON

"The Small Faces are thought to be a one-hit wonder in America, because we only had 'Itchycoo Park'" IAN McLAGAN

"Satisfaction was the song that really made the Rolling Stones, changed us from just another band into a huge, monster band. You always need one song. We weren't American, and America was a big thing and we always wanted to make it here. It was very impressive the way that song and the popularity of the band became a worldwide thing" MICK JAGGER

"I introduced Hank Marvin of The Shadows to the Italian Meazzi Echomatic Echo Unit because I couldn't find a use for it ... it contributed greatly to their sound" JOE BROWN

"Who wants to see me as Hamlet? Very few. But millions want to see me as Frankenstein so that's the one I do"

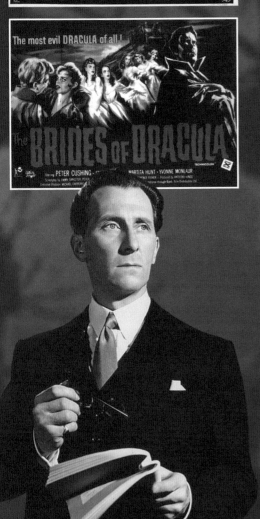

"People look at me as if I were some sort of monster, but I can't think why. In my macabre pictures, I have either been a monster-maker or a monster-destroyer, but never a monster. Actually, I'm a gentle fellow. Never harmed a fly. I love animals, and when I'm in the country I'm a keen bird watcher"

"You see I don't like to be really too commercial about things but, in this business, you've just got to be commercial, otherwise the films don't make money and you don't make films and, as long as a commodity is selling, it's silly to kill it dead"

"I hope this doesn't sound pompous, but I don't think of myself as famous. Whatever fame I've got has come through what I've done and associations of things I've done"

"As far back as I can ever remember, without really knowing I wanted to be an actor. I was always dressing up, you know, playing pretend, putting on mothers hats and things. I'm sure Freud would have something to say about that. It was very much in my blood"

PETER CUSHING

"There are many vampires in the world today. You only have to think of the film business"

"To be a legend, you've either got to be dead or excessively old"

"We don't always get the kind of work we want, but we always have a choice of whether to do it with good grace or not"

"The Dracula movies are probably some of the most famous and enduring ones there are and I am very grateful to them, for sure"

"Lon Chaney and Boris Karloff didn't like the word 'horror'. They, like I, went for the French description: 'the theatre of the fantastique'"

"I was always fascinated by fairy stories, fantasy, you know, demons, necromancers, gods and goddesses, everything that is out of our kin and out of our everyday world. I was always interested in enchantment and magicians and still am"

"I thought that people should know about the dangers of Satanism, and diabolism does exist, there's no question about it"

CHRISTOPHER LEE

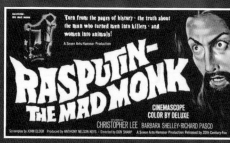

"YOU'RE ONLY SUPPOSED TO

"I was born Maurice Joseph Micklewhite. Imagine signing that autograph! You'd get a broken arm. So I changed my name to Michael Caine after Humphrey Bogart's 'The Caine Mutiny', which was playing in the theatre across from the telephone booth where I learned that I'd gotten my first TV job"

"I'm every bourgeois nightmare – a Cockney with intelligence and a million dollars"

"I come from the slums; I come from a hard background; I come from a poor family; and I was a soldier"

"At one hundred yards, volley fire present! Aim! Fire!"

"Still, a chap ought to look smart in front of the men, don't you think?"

LIEUTENANT GONVILLE BROMHEAD

BLOW THE BLOODY DOORS OFF!"

MICHAEL CAINE, THE ITALIAN JOB

"In the Sixties, everyone you knew became famous. My flatmate was Terence Stamp. My barber was Vidal Sassoon. David Hockney did the menu in a restaurant I went to. I didn't know anyone unknown who didn't become famous"

"Alfie was the first time I was above the title; the first time I became a star in America"

"In my early days, I didn't know what a good film or a bad film was, and I was trying to make some money. As it happens I was lucky. I made some good films"

"You get paid the same for a bad film as you do for a good one"

"But the whole point of the Sixties was that you had to take people as they were. If you came in with us you left your class, and colour, and religion behind, that was what the Sixties was all about"

"To boldly go
where no man has gone before"

"Space, the final frontier"
CAPTAIN JAMES T KIRK (WILLIAM SHATNER)

"Live long and prosper"
SPOCK (LEONARD NIMOY)

"Beam us up, Scotty"
CAPTAIN JAMES T KIRK (WILLIAM SHATNER)

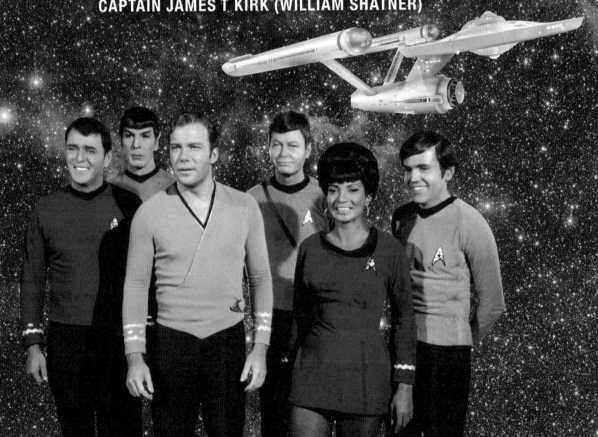

"YAAAABADABBADOOO" THE FLINTSTONES
"WHAT'S UP DOC?" BUGS BUNNY
"YOU DIABOLICAL MASTERMIND, YOU"
DIANA RIGG, Emma Peel, THE AVENGERS

"I missed so much of the Swinging Sixties by working. From 1961 to 1969, I got up at 4.30am, a car came for me at 5.30am, and I was taken to our studio at Teddington or Elstree, and we filmed until I got home at 9.30pm, five days a week"
PATRICK MACNEE, John Steed, THE AVENGERS

"TO THE BATMOBILE" ADAM WEST, BATMAN
"SOCK IT TO ME" ROWAN AND MARTIN'S LAUGH-IN
"EXTERMINATE!" THE DALEKS, DOCTOR WHO

"Television is more interesting than people. If it were not, we would have people standing in the corners of our rooms"
ALAN CORENK

"You stupid boy!"
ARTHUR LOWE
Captain Mainwaring
DAD'S ARMY

NAPOLEON SOLO:
"My name is Napoleon Solo. I'm Enforcement agent in Section 2. That's operations and enforcement"
ILLYA KURYAKIN:
"I am Illya Kuryakin. I am also an Enforcement agent. Like my friend Napoleon, I go and I do whatever I am told to by our chief"
THE MAN FROM U.N.C.L.E.

★THE★ SENSATIONAL SIXTIES

DREAM! DREAM! DREAM!

"Ooh you are awful, but I like you"
DICK EMERY

"I will not be pushed, filed, stamped, indexed, briefed, debriefed, or numbered! My life is my own!"
PATRICK McGOOHAN,
Number Six,
THE PRISONER

"Silly old moo!"
WARREN MITCHELL
Alf Garnett,
TILL DEATH DO US PART

"Yes, Master"
BARBARA EDEN
I DREAM OF JEANNIE

"Television has done much for psychiatry by spreading information about it, as well as contributing to the need for it"
ALFRED HITCHCOCK

"You rang" LURCH, THE ADDAMS FAMILY

"Book 'em, Danno"
STEVE McGARRETT, Jack Lord, HAWAII FIVE-O

"And that's the way it is"
WALTER CRONKITE, CBS EVENING NEWS

"Marsha, Marsha, Marsha"
THE BRADY BUNCH

"Who was that masked man?"
PRESIDENT ULYSSES S GRANT, THE LONE RANGER

"Hi-ho, Silver, away!"
CLAYTON MOORE, THE LONE RANGER

"The indisputable leader of the gang"
TOP CAT

"Danger, Will Robinson!"
ROBOT, LOST IN SPACE

"Here's Johnny!"
ED McMAHON, TONIGHT SHOW
starring JOHNNY CARSON

"This tape will self destruct in five seconds"
MISSION: IMPOSSIBLE

"COME ALIVE! YOU'RE IN THE PEPSI GENERATION!"

"AND ALL BECAUSE THE LADY LOVES MILK TRAY"

"THE COFFEE THAT SMELLS AS GOOD AS IT TASTES"
MAXWELL HOUSE

"BEANZ MEANZ HEINZ"

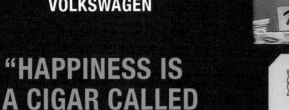

"THINK SMALL"
VOLKSWAGEN

"I'D LOVE A BABYCHAM"

"HAPPINESS IS A CIGAR CALLED HAMLET"

"AJAX CLEANS LIKE A WHITE TORNADO"

"YOU WONDER WHERE THE YELLOW WENT WHEN YOU BRUSH YOUR TEETH WITH PEPSODENT"

"PUT A TIGER IN YOUR TANK!"

"A MARS A DAY HELPS YOU WORK, REST AND PLAY"

"LET YOUR FINGERS DO THE WALKING"
YELLOW PAGES

"IT'S THE REAL THING"

"SCHHH... YOU KNOW WHO"

"PLOP, PLOP, FIZZ, FIZZ"

"GO TO WORK ON AN EGG"

"FLY THE FRIENDLY SKIES"
UNITED AIRLINES

"NOW HANDS THAT DO DISHES CAN FEEL AS SOFT AS YOUR FACE, WITH MILD GREEN FAIRY LIQUID"

"I believe in a long, prolonged, derangement of the senses in order to obtain the unknown"
JIM MORRISON

LET'S FREAK OUT TOGETHER

NOW! THE STARS OF WEST SIDE STORY TOGETHER AGAIN!
FREE GRASS
LOVE AND VIOLENCE FORM A MIND-BLOWING TRIP!!!

NICE AND EASY DOES IT

THE POLITICS OF ECSTASY BY TIMOTHY LEARY
UNABRIDGED

SMOKE a FLESH

I'D LOVE TO TURN YOU ON

"Drop acid not bombs"
UNKNOWN

"There are three side effects of acid; enhanced longterm memory, decreased short term memory, and I forget the third" TIMOTHY LEARY

"Turn on, tune in, drop out"
TIMOTHY LEARY

"The other day they asked me about mandatory drug testing. I said I believed in drug testing a long time ago. All through the Sixties I tested everything" BILL LEE

"The reason I don't smoke pot is because it facilitates ideas and heightens sensations. And I got enough shit flying through my head without smoking pot" LENNY BRUCE

"I was thinking about this the other day, and I don't really think I was suited to heavy drug behavior, to be perfectly honest. But I don't mind talking about it. It's hard to believe that you did so many drugs for so long. That's what I find really hard. And I didn't really consider it. In the Sixties, it was eating and drinking and taking drugs and having sex. It was just part of life. It wasn't really anything special. It was just a bit of a bore, really. Everyone took drugs the whole time, and you were out of it the whole time. It wasn't a special event" MICK JAGGER

"I propose, then, that everybody including the President and his and our vast hordes of generals, judges, executives and legislators of these states go to nature, find a kindly teacher or indian peyote chief or guru guide, and assay their consciousness with LSD" ALLEN GINSBERG

"Avoid all needle drugs.
The only dope worth shooting is Richard Nixon"
ABBIE HOFFMAN

"If you're not part of the solution, then you're part of the problem" ELDRIDGE CLEAVER

"The medium is the message"
MARSHALL McLUHAN

"The liberals can understand everything but people who don't understand them" LENNY BRUCE

"Sacred cows make the tastiest hamburger" ABBIE HOFFMAN

"The truth will set you free. But first, it will piss you off" GLORIA STEINEM

"Obsolescence never meant the end of anything – it's just the beginning" MARSHALL McLUHAN

ALL TIME GROOVY GREATS

"Fervour is the weapon of choice of the impotent" FRANZ FANON

"Myth is neither a lie or a confession; it is an inflexion" ROLAND BARTHES

"Boredom is always counter-revolutionary, always" GUY DEBORD

"What we need is hatred. From it our ideas are born" JEAN GENET

"My generation of the Sixties, with all our great ideas, destroyed liberalism, because of our excesses" CAMILLE PAGLIA

"The most important thing about spaceship earth, an instruction book didn't come with it" R. BUCKMINSTER FULLER

"The '60s was the end of the America that the rest of the world liked" JULIE NEWMAR

"The term 'Generation Gap' was first used in the 1960s. During that time, the younger generation, which is now referred to as the 'baby boomers', showed a significant difference in their beliefs and opinions compared to what their parents' generation projected" WILL KENTON

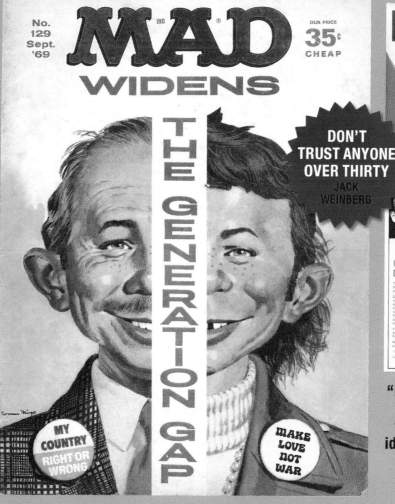

DON'T TRUST ANYONE OVER THIRTY JACK WEINBERG

"The lessons of the past are ignored and obliterated in a contemporary antagonism known as the generation gap" SPIRO T AGNEW

"I can't understand why people are frightened of new ideas. I'm frightened of the old ones" JOHN CAGE

"Our young people, in disturbing numbers, appear to reject all forms of authority, from whatever source derived, and they have taken refuge in a turbulent and inchoate nihilism whose sole objectives are destruction. I know of no time in our history when the gap between the generations has been wider or more potentially dangerous" GRAYSON KIRK, Columbia University President

"Generation gap can be a frustrating lack of communication between young and old or a useful stretch of time that separates cultures within a society, allowing them to develop their own character" WILLIAM SAFIRE

"LIVE NOW. TOMORROW, WHO KNOWS?"
CHARLES AZNAVOUR

"I have to live with both my selves as best I may" BRIGITTE BARDOT

"My motto is
'to exist is
to insist'"
JOHNNY
HALLYDAY

"I never get
bored. There isn't
enough time in
the day for me"
FRANÇOISE
HARDY

"I don't
think when I
make love"
BRIGITTE
BARDOT

"I know
what sin is"
BRIGITTE
BARDOT

VIVE LA FRANCE

"In France, the
image I had was
of a shy girl – a
poor lonely girl
and not too
good-looking.
When I went to
England, I had
another image.
I felt the journalists
were much more
interested in
my looks than
in my songs"
FRANÇOISE
HARDY

"I am a rocker and a rocker must live like a lone wolf"
JOHNNY HALLYDAY

"We need to get rid of the puzzle that we see once in a lifetime"
CHARLES AZNAVOUR

"There is a certain dignity to being French" BRIGITTE BARDOT

"OH OUI, JE T'AIME!"

SERGE GAINSBOURG

"I am incapable of mediocrity"

"I've succeeded at everything except life"

"I know my limits. That's why I'm beyond"

"I will compose to decomposition"

"Physical love is hopeless"

"I'm a rusty bullet shot and I will die of tetanus"

"Hugs and punches in the mouth are the thick and thin strokes of love"

"Love without philosophizing is like having a quick coffee"

"The mask falls, the man remains, and the hero vanishes"

"If I had to choose between a woman and a final cigarette, I would choose the cigarette. You can throw it away easier!"

"Love is blind and his cane is pink"

"We take women for what they are not and leave them for what they are"

"If I were God, I might be the only one not to believe in me"

"I like the night, I have clearer ideas in the dark"

"The man created gods. The opposite is yet to be proved"

"Snobbery is a bubble of champagne which hesitates between burping and farting"

"Ugliness is in a way superior to beauty because it lasts"

"Cinema is the most beautiful fraud in the world"

"Film is truth 24 times a second, and every cut is a lie"

"If direction is a look, montage is a heartbeat. To foresee is the characteristic of both; but what one seeks to foresee in space, the other seeks in time"

"Cinema is capitalism in it's purest form... there is only one solution – turn one's back on American Cinema"

"Art is not a reflection of reality, it is the reality of a reflection"

"Europe has memories. America has T-shirts"

"One must confront vague ideas with clear images"

"To be or not to be. That's not really a question"

"I pity the French Cinema because it has no money. I pity the American Cinema because it has no ideas"

JEAN-LUC GODARD

"When sex gets problematic, the totalitarianist walks in"

"I like the idea of making films about ostensibly absolutely nothing. I like the irrelevant, the tangential, the sidebar excursion to nowhere that suddenly becomes revelatory"

"The world isn't a sad place, it's just big"

"First there was Greek civilization. Then there was the Renaissance. Now we're entering the age of the Ass"

"When you go to the cinema you look up, when you watch television you look down"

"There is no point in having sharp images when you've fuzzy ideas"

"THE MORE BOMBERS, THE LESS ROOM FOR DOVES OF PEACE"
NIKITA KHRUSHCHEV

"I worked for MI6 in the Sixties, during the great witch-hunts, when the shared paranoia of the Cold War gripped the services"
JOHN LE CARRE

"Well, I actually grew up in the Sixties. I feel very lucky, actually, that that was my slice of time that I was dealt. Let's remember that the real motivation in the Sixties, and even in the Fifties, was the Cold War" ANN DRYUAN

"The trouble with a Cold War is that it doesn't take too long before it becomes heated"
ANTHONY T HINCKS

"All free men, wherever they live, are citizens of Berlin, and therefore, as a free man, I take pride in the words 'Ich bin ein Berliner'"
JOHN F KENNEDY

"The American foreign policy trauma of the Sixties was caused by applying valid principles to unsuitable conditions"
HENRY KISSINGER

"In 1960, the United States and the Soviet Union were locked into an idealistically-driven Cold War, pitting the Capitalistic West against the Communistic East. Cuba, unable to be self-sufficient, had to pick a side. With the United States putting economic pressure onto the relatively small country, Castro did the only thing his pride would allow. Voicing disdain for his neighbor to the north, Castro proclaimed that his ideological views paralleled those of the USSR. Meeting with the Soviet Premier Anastas Mikoyan, Castro agreed to provide the USSR with food and sugar, in return for a monetary infusion amounting to a $100 million loan, as well as industrial goods, crude oil and fertilizers. Castro's first public admission that his revolution was socialistic was during his speech honoring the people killed in the air strikes of April 15, 1961, during the Bay of Pigs operation. The Cuban government then took over all the banks, except two Canadian ones.

On October 26, 1963, Nikita Khrushchev contacted President Kennedy and offered to remove the missiles from Cuba in exchange for a promise that the United States would not invade the Island Nation. A day later on October 27th, Khrushchev sent a letter proposing that the Soviet Union would dismantle their missiles in Cuba, if the Americans reciprocated by removing their missile installations in Turkey. Although the cold war was far from over, both sides knowing how close they came from an all-out conflict, had a "hot line" installed between Washington and Moscow, hoping to prevent any similar situations in the future. The hot line is sometimes called the red telephone, even though it wasn't even a telephone, nor was it red"

CAPTAIN HANK BRACKER

"A man may die, nations may rise

"The real 1960s began on the afternoon of November 22, 1963. It came to seem that Kennedy's murder opened some malign trap door in American culture, and the wild bats flapped out" LANCE MORROW

"We believe that if men have the talent to invent new machines that put men out of work, they have the talent to put those men back to work"

"My father always told me that all businessmen were sons of bitches, but I never believed it till now"

"Mothers all want their sons to grow up to be President, but they don't want them to become politicians in the process"

"And so, my fellow Americans, ask not what your country can do for you; ask what you can do for your country"

JOHN F KENNEDY

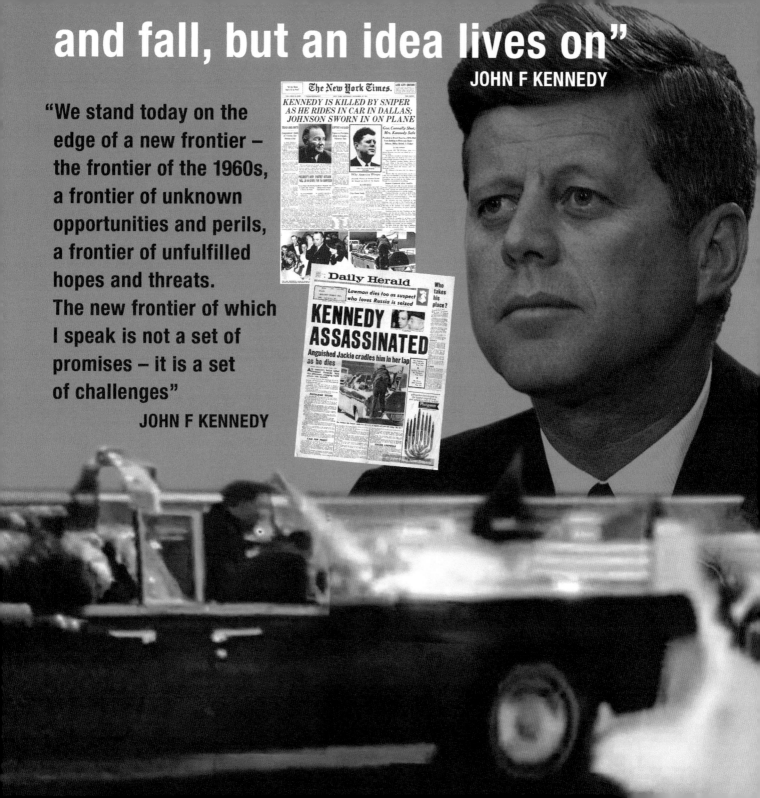

and fall, but an idea lives on"
JOHN F KENNEDY

"We stand today on the edge of a new frontier – the frontier of the 1960s, a frontier of unknown opportunities and perils, a frontier of unfulfilled hopes and threats. The new frontier of which I speak is not a set of promises – it is a set of challenges"

JOHN F KENNEDY

"I HAVE A

"We must learn to live together as brothers or perish together as fools"

"A riot is the language of the unheard"

"Freedom is never voluntarily given by the oppressor; it must be demanded by the oppressed"

"The ultimate measure of a man is not where he stands in moments of comfort and convenience, but where he stands at times of challenge and controversy"

"The Negro's great stumbling block in the drive toward freedom is not the White Citizens Councillor or the Ku Klux Klanner, but the white moderate who is more devoted to order than to justice"

DREAM..."

MARTIN LUTHER KING

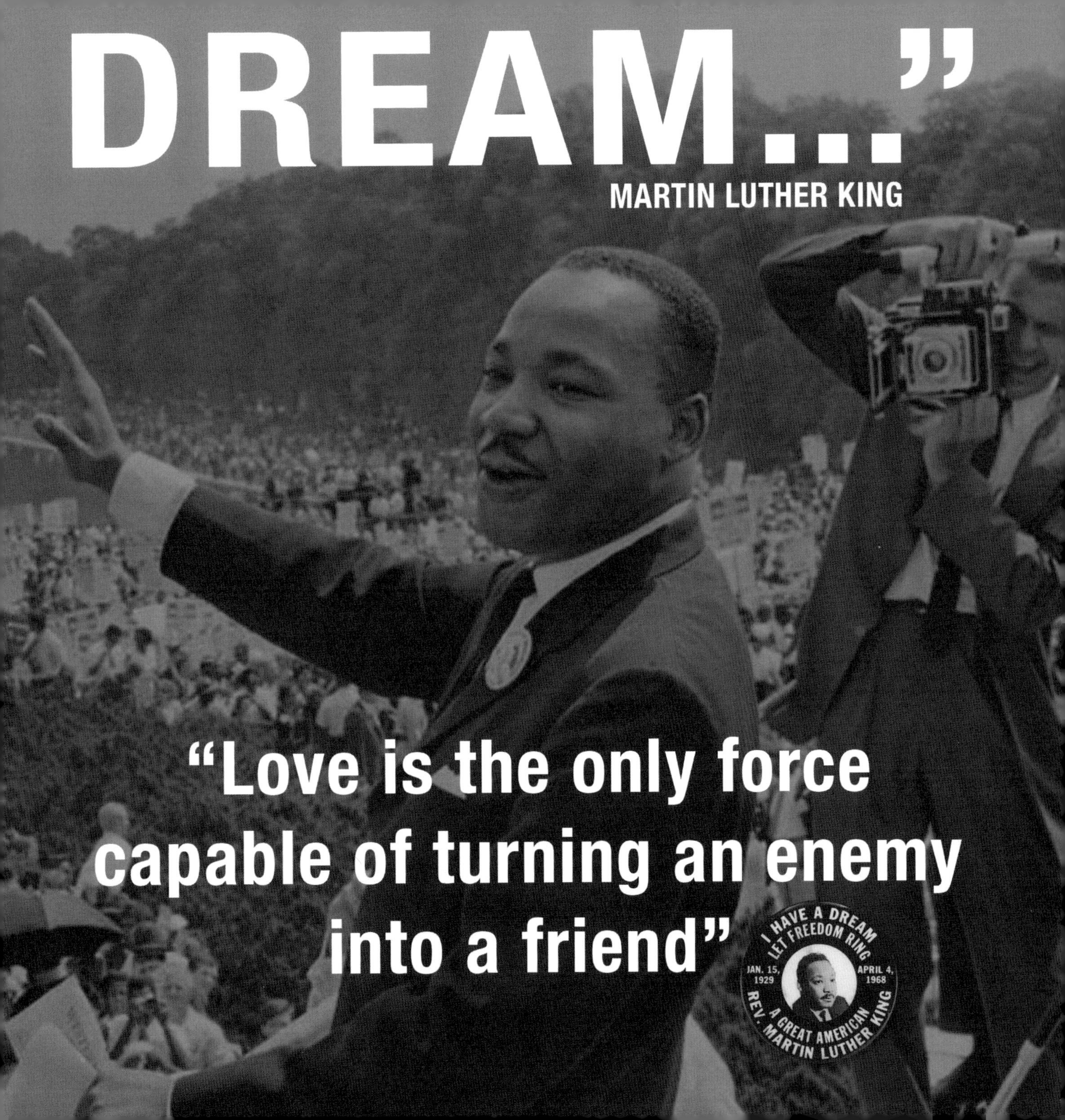

"Love is the only force capable of turning an enemy into a friend"

I HAVE A DREAM
LET FREEDOM RING
JAN. 15, 1929
APRIL 4, 1968
REV. MARTIN LUTHER KING
A GREAT AMERICAN

"A WOMAN NEEDS A MAN LIKE A FISH NEEDS A BICYCLE"
IRINA DUNN

"Birth control is an ethical necessity... because it places in our (women's) hands a new instrument of self-realization. It gives us control"
MARGARET SANGER

WOMEN OF THE WORLD UNITE

"The connections between and among women are the most feared, the most problematic, and the most potentially transforming force on the planet"
ADRIENNE RICH

"NO WOMAN GETS AN ORGASM FROM SHINING THE KITCHEN FLOOR"

"Woman is seen only in terms of her sexual role, the barrier to the realization of her full potential. It is ridiculous to tell girls to keep quiet when they enter a new field, or an old one, so the men will not notice they are (there). Some women in their forties and fifties still remembered painfully giving up those dreams, but most of the younger women no longer even thought about them"

"Each suburban wife struggles with it alone. As she made the beds, shopped for groceries, matched slipcover material, ate peanut butter sandwiches with her children, chauffeured Cub Scouts and Brownies, lay beside her husband at night – she was afraid to ask even of herself the silent question, 'Is this all?'"

BETTY FRIEDAN

"Let us begin the revolution and let us begin it with love: all of us, black, white, and gold, male and female, have it within our power to create a world we could bear out of the desert we inhabit, for we hold our very fate in our hands" KATE MILLET

"You must strive to multiply bread so that it suffices for the tables of mankind, and not rather favor an artificial control of birth, which would be irrational, in order to diminish the number of guests at the banquet of life" POPE PAUL VI

THE FEMININE MYSTIQUE

BETTY FRIEDAN

"EVERYTHING I LEARNED I LEARNED FROM THE MOVIES"
AUDREY HEPBURN

"If only every man who sees my films did not get the impression he can make love to me, I would be a lot happier"
BRIGITTE BARDOT

"I dress for women and I undress for men"
ANGIE DICKINSON

★THE★
SENSATIONAL
SIXTIES

GIRLS! GIRLS! GIRLS!

"Big girls need big diamonds"
LIZ TAYLOR

"Fame, I mean, it's like a bubble, in a way. It's like something glittery, and it goes, and it can be forgotten fast"
VERUSCHKA VON LEHNDORFF

"Being an actress is to be in tune with the fantasies of a man. What woman never dreamt of that?"
JEANNE MOREAU

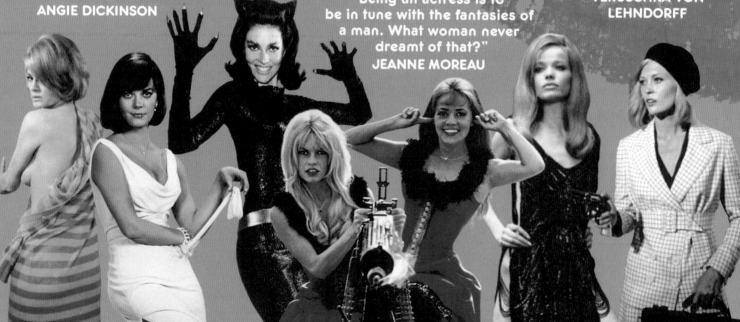

"HAPPY BIRTHDAY MR PRESIDENT, HAPPY BIRTHDAY TO YOU"
MARILYN MONROE

"Almost every girl falls in love with the wrong man. I suppose it's part of growing up"
NATALIE WOOD

"I'm not overweight, I'm just nine inches too short"
SHELLEY WINTERS

"I sort of dropped the ball after Bonnie and Clyde"
FAYE DUNAWAY

"A Latin teacher told me I might make a good actress, and that stuck in my memory. I did some modeling, and Polanski gave me that small part"
JACQUELINE BISSET

"I'm magnificent! I'm 5'11" and I weigh 135 pounds, and I look like a racehorse"
JULIE NEWMAR

"I was utilized because I have a certain face that works well in cinema, and I'm used to making myself look as good as possible"
JULIE CHRISTIE

"I want women to be liberated and still be able to have a nice ass and shake it"
SHIRLEY MACLAINE

"Some of my best leading men have been dogs and horses"
LIZ TAYLOR

"WAVES ARE NOT MEASURED IN FEET AND INCHES,

RIDE THE WILD SURF

TEN TOES SURF BOARD

PRAY FOR SURF

SALT CREEK, CALIFORNIA, SINCE 1919
BIRDS ORIGINAL SURF WAX
ALL NATURAL INGREDIENTS

"I like surfers.
Their imagery, it's great"
RAY DAVIES

"Ever since our Surfin' Safari began in the early 1960s, the relationship with THE BEACH BOYS and water has been synonymous. SURFIN', CATCH A WAVE and SURFIN' USA are songs which capture the feelings of being out in the water without a care in the world, living a dream so many long to live, no matter where they are from" MIKE LOVE

The Beach Boys
SURFIN'
ORIGINAL RECORDINGS

THEY ARE MEASURED IN INCREMENTS OF FEAR"
BUZZY TRENT

DICK DALE

ALL TIME
Instrumental
★GREATS★

"SURF MUSIC is actually just the sound of the waves played on a guitar: that wet, splashy sound"

"When I was 18 at the Santa Ana River Jetty is where I put my first board in the water that I ever got from Joe Quigg. I was just riding the whitewater in, and I was just in heaven"

"The kids called me **KING OF THE SURF GUITAR.** I surfed sunup to sundown"

"When my guitar was growling, playing surf beat, you could hear it; you could feel it"

"I used to surf up in Ventura County at Silver Strand; plus, I've played up there many times"

"Surf music is played through a Showman amp with a Stratocaster guitar"

"Surfers were the ones who named all my songs. They'd yell out the names and we just kept 'em"

"Hey, hey, LBJ, how many boys did you kill today?"
CHANTING PROTESTERS PICKETING THE WHITE HOUSE

"This war has already stretched the generation gap so wide that it threatens to pull the country apart"
SENATOR FRANK CHURCH

"Our purpose in Vietnam is to prevent the success of aggression. It is not conquest, it is not empire, it is not foreign bases, it is not domination. It is, simply put, just to prevent the forceful conquest of South Vietnam by North Vietnam" PRESIDENT LYNDON B JOHNSON

"Yippies, Hippies, Yahoos, Black Panthers, lions and tigers alike – I would swap the whole damn zoo for the kind of young Americans I saw in Vietnam"
SPIRO T AGNEW

"Without censorship, things can get terribly confused in the public mind"
GENERAL WILLIAM WESTMORELAND

"I am not going to lose Vietnam. I am not going to be the President who saw South East Asia go the way of China"
PRESIDENT LYNDON B JOHNSON

"In the previous administration, we Americanized the war in Vietnam. In this administration, we are Vietnamizing the search for peace"
PRESIDENT RICHARD M NIXON

"I was proud of the youths who opposed the war in Vietnam because they were my babies"
BENJAMIN SPOCK

"North Vietnam cannot defeat or humiliate the United States, only Americans can do that"
RICHARD M NIXON

"It's silly talking about how many years we will have to spend in the jungles of Vietnam when we could pave the whole country and put parking stripes on it and still be home for Christmas"
RONALD REAGAN

"Television brought the brutality of war into the comfort of the living room. Vietnam was lost in the living rooms of America – not on the battlefields of Vietnam" MARSHALL McLUHAN

"Vietnam was what we had instead of happy childhoods"
MICHAEL HERR

"Vietnam has changed America. It has divided and made people think. There's a lot of opposition – much more than you think, because all the opposition is laughed at in American magazines. It's made to look ridiculous. But there is real opposition. Before, Americans used to accept everything, my country right or wrong. But now a lot of people are saying my country should be right, not wrong"
MICK JAGGER

"The Sixties was like coitus interruptus. The only thing we didn't pull out of was Vietnam"
LILY TOMLIN

"I think a long protracted war will disclose our weakness, not our strength"
GEORGE W BALL
DEPUTY SECRETARY OF STATE

"**Everybody moving, everybody grooving. People got the London look**" HERMAN'S HERMITS

THE COOLEST GUYS IN TOWN

"**Fashion is as profound and critical a part of the social life of man as sex, and is made up of the same ambivalent mixture of irresistible urges and inevitable taboos**"
RENE KONIG

"**Trendy is the last stage before tacky**" KARL LAGERFELD

"**Fashion is what you adopt when you don't know who you are**" QUENTIN CRISP

"They seek him here, they seek him there
His clothes are loud, but never square
It will make or break him so he's got to buy the best
'Cause he's dedicated follower of fashion

And when he does his little rounds
'Round of the boutiques of London Town
Eagerly pursuing all the latest fads and trends
'Cause he's dedicated follower of fashion" RAY DAVIES

"There we were in the middle of a sexual revolution,
wearing clothes that guaranteed we wouldn't get laid"
DENIS LEARY

"It didn't matter how quickly
everything fell to bits. The clothes
weren't meant to last, but to
dazzle. Their shops, blaring pop
music and vying with each other
for the campest window and
decor, spread the length of
Carnaby Street and its environs"
GEORGE MELLY

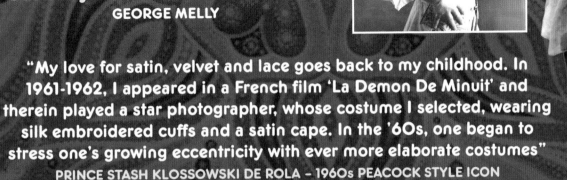

"My love for satin, velvet and lace goes back to my childhood. In
1961-1962, I appeared in a French film 'La Demon De Minuit' and
therein played a star photographer, whose costume I selected, wearing
silk embroidered cuffs and a satin cape. In the '60s, one began to
stress one's growing eccentricity with ever more elaborate costumes"
PRINCE STASH KLOSSOWSKI DE ROLA – 1960s PEACOCK STYLE ICON

"IF YOU'RE GOING TO SAN FRANCISCO, BE

"In a gentle way, you can shake the world"
MAHATMA GANDHI

WHAT A CRAZY WORLD!

"ALL YOU NEED IS
LOVE"
THE BEATLES

"When LOVE played the still hipper Whisky A Go-Go, further west along Sunset, Arther Lee claims they 'started the whole hippy thing' in tandem with an in-crowd of freaks led by aging beatnik sculptor Vito Paulekas" **BARNEY HOSKYNS**

SURE TO WEAR SOME FLOWERS IN YOUR HAIR"
SCOTT McKENZIE

"Hippy is an establishment label for a profound, invisible, underground, evolutionary process. For every visible hippy, barefoot, beflowered, beaded, there are a thousand invisible members of the turned-on underground. Persons whose lives are tuned in to their inner vision who are dropping out of the TV comedy of American Life" TIMOTHY LEARY

"What am I thinking about? I'm trying to figure out where I am between the established politicians and the radicals, between cops and hoods, tax collectors and vandals. I'm not a Tax-Free, not a Hippie-Yippie – I must be a Bippie-in-the-middle" JACK KEROUAC

"When I think of my childhood, I see my mother, the complete Sixties parent, decked in purple frappe silk kaftans, the acidic smell of newly stripped pine mingling with incense" HAMISH BOWLES

"Peace is not the destination. Peace is the way" UNKNOWN

"Hippies are so phoney and fake" GEORGE HARRISON

"You're either on the bus, or off the bus" KEN KESEY

"OTIS REDDING WAS LIKE SEEING A GOD ONSTAGE"

BOB WEIR, GRATEFUL DEAD

"Sunshine came softly through my a-window today. Could've tripped out easy a-but I've a-changed my ways. It'll take time, I know it but in a while" DONOVAN

LET THE SUNSHINE IN

MONTEREY
INTERNATIONAL POP FESTIVAL

FROM THE EAST VILLAGE, NY **SIMON & GARFUNKEL**	FROM LONDON, ENGLAND **THE JIMI HENDRIX EXPERIENCE**	FOLK SENSATIONS! **MAMAS & PAPAS**
GET 8 MILES HIGH WITH **THE BYRDS**	ENGLAND'S FINEST **THE WHO**	THE VOICE OF SOUL **OTIS REDDING**
THE UNIQUE SOUND OF **JEFFERSON AIRPLANE**	FROM PALO ALTO CALIFORNIA **GRATEFUL DEAD**	**BUFFALO SPRINGFIELD** WITH DAVID CROSBY
ERIC BURDON & THE ANIMALS		

PLUS RAVI SHANKAR·CANNED HEAT·BIG BROTHER & THE HOLDING CO.·SCOTT MCKENZIE AND MARY MORE

JUNE 16-18 MONTEREY COUNTY FAIRGROUNDS
TICKETS $2.50,$4.00 & $6.50

"I was admired by all these hippies, and it was wonderful playing at Monterey and Woodstock, performing for half a million people" RAVI SHANKAR

"Flowers everywhere… it was true flower power. The vibe was beautiful. The music was fantastic. That to me was the purest, most beautiful moment of the whole '60s trip" DENNIS HOPPER

"Drugs were everywhere at Monterey Pop, as was par for the course in the '60s and the Summer of Love. In fact, Los Angeles band The Association kicked off the festival with *Along Comes Mary*, a thinly veiled salute to marijuana. But the festival wasn't what the Monterey police force expected" LOU ADLER

"THE MONTEREY POP FESTIVAL WAS THE EPITOME OF THE SUMMER OF LOVE" RICHARD HAVERS

"We were doing the Monterey Pop Festival, which I produced with Lou Adler, and the town of Monterey was sort of frightened by the thought of two hundred and fifty thousand hippies coming" JOHN PHILLIPS

"Usually I just did my films by myself. The idea of having to do a concert film with four or five or six cameramen was something I never even thought about doing before. As a result, Monterey Pop was made by 'kinda letting everybody go out and do whatever they thought a concert film should be'" D. A. PENNEBAKER

"It didn't take long for them to have flowers in their hair and in their helmets and flowers on their guns. The changeover from what they were told was going to happen to what actually happened in Monterey was very special" LOU ADLER

"Hendrix is a one-man explosion. What he does to a guitar could get him arrested" KEITH ALTHAM

"The highlights included Joplin's incendiary performance, The Who's Pete Townshend smashing his guitar during *My Generation*, and Jimi Hendrix burning his guitar during *Wild Thing!*" GARY BONGIOVANNI

"This is really a great scene here. All the kids are so nice. The people are so polite and just come up and talk to me and say they like the way I'm dressed" BRIAN JONES

"Sex is a bad thing because it rumples the clothes"
JACKIE KENNEDY

"You have to remember this was the '60s, when climbing was dangerous and sex was safe"
YVON CHOUINARD

"Sex is like washing your face – just something you do because you have to. Sex without love is absolutely ridiculous"
SOPHIA LOREN

"I honestly don't understand the big fuss made over nudity and sex in films, it's silly"
SHARON TATE

"Sex is hardly ever just about sex"
SHIRLEY McCLAINE

"I'm proud of my breasts, every woman should be"
ANITA EKBERG

"Beyond the beauty, the sex, the titillation. The surface, there is a human being and that has to emerge"
JEANNE MOREAU

"After a decade of sleeping around pretty indiscriminately, girls of the '60s eventually became fairly jaded about sex'
VIRGINIA IRONSIDE

"The only burning passion I'm sure I have, is the passion for sex"
ROBERT CRUMB

"To be honest, I mainly remember the '60s as an endless round of miserable promiscuity, a time when it often seemed easier, and believe it or not, more polite, to sleep with a man than to chuck him out of your flat"
VIRGINIA IRONSIDE

"Sex is. There is nothing more to be done about it. Sex builds no roads, writes no novels and sex certainly gives no meaning to anything in life but itself"
GORE VIDAL

"For flavour. Instant sex will never supersede the stuff you have to peel and cook"
QUENTIN CRISP

"Sex is full of lies. The body tries to tell the truth. But, it's usually too battered with rules to be heard, and bound with pretences so it can hardly move. We cripple ourselves with lies"
JIM MORRISON

"Being a sex symbol was rather like being a convict"
RAQUEL WELCH

"DISCO-DYKES DANCE IN A DEN OF DEPRAVITY"
LESBIANS A GO GO – L J BROWN

"SIN-SICK MINDS DEMANDED SHAM TORTURED BODIES!"
THE PAIN LUSTERS – DON ELLIOTT

"SULTRY AS THE SOUTHERN SUN. WILD DESIRES THROBBED
IN HER PASSIONATE SOUL"
THE WARM FLESH – VINCENT KEITH

"HER PAGAN DESIRES VIOLATED EVEN THE LOOSE
MORAL CODE OF THE MARSHLANDS"
SWAMP BRED – GEORGE E SMITH

"TEENAGE LUSTS ON A RAMPAGE OF SHARP KNIVES AND
EASY GIRLS – BLOOD AND PASSION IN A GUTTER WORLD"
SEX JUNGLE – DON ELLIOTT

"TO FOOL THE WORLD, THEY MARRIED. FOR JOAN
LOVED WOMEN... AND MARK PREFERRED MEN!"
THE THIRD SEX – ARTEMIS SMITH

"TWISTED HUNGERS GAVE THEM PASSION PLEASURE!"
SINDUSTRY – JOHN DEXTER

"THE TOWN WAS WILD, AND THE WOMEN WILDER!"
JAZZMEN IN NUDE TOWN – BOB TRALINS

"SHE RODE HIGH, WIDE AND WICKED ON
A MERRY GO ROUND OF SEX"
ANY MAN WILL DO – GREG HAMILTON

"TWISTED PASSIONS RULED HER WANTON BODY"
SEX BAIT – DON ELLIOTT

"A LUSH NYMPH GOT HER KICKS FROM TEASING MEN"
PERVERTED LOVER – BILL LAUREN

"DANNY'S GIRLS COULDN'T BE BEAT! BUY THEM.
SELL THEM. WIN THEM... EVEN TAKE THEM FOR NOTHING...
JUST KEEP THEM SATISFIED!"
TONIGHT SHE'S YOURS – JAY HART

"A WILD YANK ON THE PROWL IN THE PASSION
JUNGLES OF THE ORIENT"
MALAY MISTRESS – CLYDE ALLISON

THE
COOLEST
SWINGERS
IN
TOWN

"You've got the guilt anyway.
Don't waste it"
BOB SANDERS (ROBERT CULP)

"Miss Keeler and I were on friendly terms. There was no impropriety whatsoever in my aquaintanceship with Miss Keeler" JOHN PROFUMO

"I won't say I didn't like it at the time, the sex, that is, because I wouldn't have let him do it at all if that had been the case" CHRISTINE KEELER

"I am notorious. I will go down in history as another Lady Hamilton" MANDY RICE DAVIES

"I'm sorry to disappoint the vulture... I feel the day is lost. The ritual sacrifice is demanded and I cannot face it" STEPHEN WARD

"I was determined that no British Government should be brought down by two tarts" HAROLD MACMILLAN Prime Minister

"Well, he would, wouldn't he?" MANDY RICE DAVIES

28 June 1963, appearing as a witness in the trial of Stephen Ward, in reply to the defence barrister putting it to her that one of the men on a certain list, Lord Astor, had denied any involvement with her. The court burst into laughter

"I give my daughter what I really didn't have as a kid: all the silly dumb, extravagant, non-functional toys I can force on her. She probably wants an encyclopaedia" LENNY BRUCE

"Perhaps the most famous game of all time was 1960s classic Twister. Released in 1966, the game caused some controversy when it first came out. Twister was the first game to truly utilise the human body. As a result, some puritans and game competitors maintained that it was 'selling sex in a box'" DAN FLETCHER

"I've always been afraid of people playing their life away with too many toys" RAY BRADBURY

"Our inventions are wont to be pretty toys, which distract our attention from serious things. They are but improved means to an unimproved end" HENRY DAVID THOREAU

"Let's play house" "Tell me a story" CHATTY CATHY

"The first prototype G I JOE action figure was hand carved in 1963 by the designer, Don Levine. G I JOE was initially a massive success and Hasbro expanded the line throughout the '60s, reimagining Joe as an astronaut, a deep-sea diver and a Green Beret. But the outcry over American involvement in Vietnam dampened enthusiasm for a camo-clad action figure, so Hasbro gave Joe an honorable discharge" DAN FLETCHER

"You have no idea how humiliating it was, as a boy, to suddenly have all your clothes, your toys, snatched by the bailiff. I mean we were a middle-class family, it's not as if it was happening up and down the street. It made me ashamed, I felt dirty" JOHN LE CARRE

"Alf Ramsey was clever. He didn't play exciting football but it was functional, pragmatic, safe – he wanted to win" STUART HALL

"Some people are on the pitch!
They think it's all over!
It is now, it's four!"
KENNETH WOLSTENHOME

"We have still to produce our best and this is not possible until we meet the right sort of opponents, and that is a team that comes out to play football and not act like animals" ALF RAMSEY (after Argentina's skipper Antonio Rattin had been sent off for 'violence of the tongue')

THE FIRST MAN TO BE SENT OFF!

"WE'RE ALL GOING ON A

"Oh, when the sun beats down and burns the tar up on the roof
And your shoes get so hot you wish your tired feet were fire proof
Under the boardwalk, down by the sea, yeah
On a blanket with my baby is where I'll be"
THE DRIFTERS

HOT SUMMER HITS

"IT WAS AN ITSY BITSY TEENIE WEENIE YELLOW POLKA-DOT BIKINI"
BRIAN HYLAND

"I'm gonna raise a fuss, I'm gonna raise a holler
About a workin' all summer just to try to earn a dollar
Every time I call my baby, and ask to get a date
My boss says, "no dice son, you gotta work late"
Sometimes I wonder what I'm a gonna do
But there ain't no cure for the summertime blues"
THE BEACH BOYS

"Everybody's hustlin' just to have a little scene
When I say we'll be cool I think that you know what I mean
We stood on a beach at sunset, do you remember when?
I know a beach where, baby, a-it never ends
When you've made your mind up forever to be mine"
DONOVAN

SUMMER HOLIDAY"
CLIFF RICHARD

"Let's have a beach party, yay!

Beer cans, pots and pans
Cigarette butts and paper cuts
A beach party's goin' on

Well, beach balls, volley balls
Ice cubes and inner-tubes
A beach party's goin' on

Now people if you wanna
I'll have a ball
Just listen listen to me
There's a crazy party going on
Down by that sandy sea

Well hot dogs, burning logs
Ice cream and pork and beans
A beach party's goin' on

Well surfboards,
extension cords
French fries and pizza pies
A beach party's goin' on

Now children if you want
I'll have a ball
Just listen listen to me
There's a crazy party going on
Down by that sandy sea

Sand crabs, ho-dance
Orange peels and rods and reels
A beach party's goin' on

Well guitars, mustard jars
Hand-holding and mud holes
A beach party's goin' on

Well, hot dog buns, bongo drums
Potato chips and onion dips
A beach party's goin' on
A beach party's goin' on"
DAVE YORK

It's what happens when 10,000 kids meet on 5,000 Beach Blankets!

CUMMINGS
MALONE · AVALON · FUNICELLO · ASHLEY · AMSTERDAM · SIX · DICK DALE AND THE DEL-TONES

American International Pictures

BEACH PARTY
IN COLOR AND PANAVISION

WILLIAM ASHER · LOU RUSOFF · JAMES H. NICHOLSON and SAMUEL Z. ARKOFF · Les Baxter

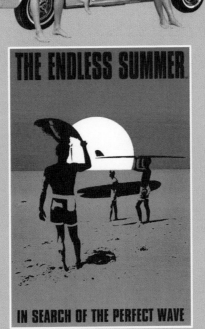

THE ENDLESS SUMMER
IN SEARCH OF THE PERFECT WAVE

"V-A-C-A-T-I-O-N in the summer sun
Put away the books, we're out of school
The weather's warm but we'll play it cool
We're on vacation, havin' lots of fun
V-A-C-A-T-I-O-N in the summer sun
We're gonna grab a bite at the pizza stand
Write love letters in the sand
We're on vacation and the world is ours
V-A-C-A-T-I-O-N under summer stars"
CONNIE FRANCIS

"Sunny
Yesterday my life was filled with rain
Sunny
You smiled at me and really eased the pain
Now the dark days are gone, and the bright
days are here
My sunny one shines so sincere
Sunny one so true, I love you"
BOBBY HEBB

"Here comes summer
School is out, oh happy day
Here comes summer
I'm gonna grab my girl and run away
Here comes summer
We'll go swimmin' every day
Oh, let the sun shine bright on my
happy summer home"
JERRY KELLER

"Walking in the sand
(Remember) walking hand-in-hand
(Remember) the night was so exciting
(Remember) smile was so inviting
(Remember) then he touched my cheek
(Remember) with his fingertips
Softly, softly we'd meet with our lips"
THE SHANGRI-LAS

"T-shirts, cut-offs, and a pair of thongs
We've been having fun all summer long"
THE BEACH BOYS

"THE NAME'S BOND. JAMES BOND" SEAN CONNERY

"DO YOU EXPECT ME TO TALK?"
"NO MR BOND, I EXPECT YOU TO DIE"

"VODKA MARTINI, SHAKEN, NOT STIRRED"

"My name is Pussy Galore"
HONOR BLACKMAN

"Flattery will get you nowhere, but don't stop trying"
MISS MONEYPENNY, LOIS MAXWELL

"When do you sleep, 007?"
M, BERNARD LEE

"He was the most extraordinary man I ever knew. It was my privilege to know him and make him known to the world. He was a poet, a scholar and a mighty warrior. He was also the most shameless exhibitionist since Barnum and Bailey"
LAWRENCE OF ARABIA

"Tell me, uh, how do you find America?"
"Turn left at Greenland"
A HARD DAY'S NIGHT

"That one convict's been a thorn in my side for 35 years. But I'll give him one thing – he's never lied to me"
BIRDMAN OF ALCATRAZ

"That's the way it crumbles, cookie-wise" THE APARTMENT

"Feed me!"
THE LITTLE SHOP OF HORRORS

"Hey, Boo"
TO KILL A MOCKINGBIRD

"Then you mean, all this time we could've been friends?"
WHAT EVER HAPPENED TO BABY JANE?

"Infamy! Infamy! They've all got it in for me" CARRY ON CLEO

"Mama, face it. I was the slut of all-time"
BUTTERFIELD 8

"The rain in Spain stays mainly in the plain!"
"By George, she's got it!"
MY FAIR LADY

"God is dead! Satan lives! The year is One, the year is One!"
ROSEMARY'S BABY

"Fat man, you shoot a great game of pool"
"So do you, Fast Eddie"
THE HUSTLER

"Hello, gorgeous"
FUNNY GIRL

"Dr Hombards, we are vundering if anybody instructed Lolita in the vacts of life? ... You see, Lolita is a sweet little child, but the onset of maturity seems to be giving her a certain amount of trouble... Dr Hombards, to you she's still za liddle girl what is cradled in zee arms. But to dose boys over dare at Beardsley High she is a lovely girl, you know, mit mit mit mit mit de sving, you know, und zat jazz. She has got a curvature zat zat they take a lot of notice of"

DR ZEMPF

"There's been such a revolution in Hollywood's treatment of sex over the past few years. It's easy to forget that, when I first became interested in Lolita, a lot of people felt that such a film couldn't be made – or at least couldn't be shown"

STANLEY KUBRICK

★THE★ SENSATIONAL SIXTIES

BABY! BABY! BABY!

BILD-LILLI

"Every little girl needed a doll through which to project herself into her dream of her future"

RUTH HANDLER
Creator of Barbie, who discovered Bild-Lilli on a European vacation to Germany. She pitched the idea to Mattel and the rest is history

"With the rabbit as our emblem, when we got to the point in 1960 of opening the first Playboy Club... one of our executives suggested the possibility of a bunny costume. We tried it out, and I made some modifications – added the cuffs and the bow tie and collar – and the bunny was born" HUGH HEFNER

"Sex is the driving force on the planet. We should embrace it, not see it as the enemy"

"'Playboy' was not a sex magazine as far as I was concerned. Sex was simply part of the total package; I was trying to bring sex into the fold of a healthy lifestyle"

"The women's movement, from my point of view, was part of the larger sexual revolution that 'Playboy' had played such a large part in. The reality is that the major beneficiaries of the sexual revolution are women"

"The major civilizing force in the world is not religion, it is sex"

"Someone once asked, 'What's your best pickup line?' I said, 'My best pickup line is Hi, my name is Hugh Hefner'"

"Part of the concept behind the magazine was breaking barriers. And it wasn't just a sexual thing. It was racial and doing the things that were right. And in the process, that set 'Playboy' apart"

"Picasso had his pink period and his blue period. I am in my blonde period right now"

"Being attacked by right-wing Christians did not bother me. Being attacked by liberal feminists did"

"Men's magazines in the period immediately after World War II were almost all outdoor-oriented. They were connected to some extent in the male bonding that came out of a war... And what I tried to create was a magazine for the indoor guy, but focused specifically on the single life: in other words, the period of bachelorhood before you settle down"

"I'M ACTUALLY A VERY MORAL GUY" HUGH HEFNER

"Like a true nature's child
We were born, born to be wild"
STEPPENWOLF

BORN TO BE WILD

"My wild love is crazy
She screams like a bird
She moans like a cat
When she wants to be heard
My wild love went ridin'
She rode for an hour
She rode and she rested
And then she rode on
Ride, c'mon"
THE DOORS

"You're lost in this great big city
Go back home where you belong
Not one familiar face, ain't it a pity
Go back home where you belong
Oh, runaway child running wild
You better go back home where
you belong" THE TEMPTATIONS

"Wild thing, you make my heart sing
You make everything groovy, wild thing" THE TROGGS

"Ohhh Yeah I'm a Wild One; I'm gonna keep a shakin'
I'm gonna keep a movin' baby; Don't you cramp my style
I'm real wild child!" JERRY LEE LEWIS

"EXCUSE ME WHILE I KISS THE SKY"

JIMI HENDRIX

When I die, I want people to play my music, go wild and freak out and do anything they want to do

"The time I burned my guitar it was like a sacrifice. You only sacrifice the things you love. I love my guitar"

"I've been imitated so well I've heard people copy my mistakes"

"Music makes me high on stage, and that's the truth. It's like being almost addicted to music"

"When I die, just keep playing the records"

"I wish they'd had electric guitars in cotton fields back in the good old days. A whole lot of things would've been straightened out"

"When things get too heavy, just call me helium, the lightest known gas to man"

"Music is my religion"

"Imagination is the key to my lyrics. The rest is painted with a little science fiction"

"When Presley's fans think of him now, it's the indelible image of the King decked out in black leather in 1968, ruling his kingdom like the self-proclaimed Tiger Man he was" KORY GROW, ROLLING STONE

"TODAY'S TEARDROPS ARE TOMORROW'S RAINBOWS" RICKY NELSON

HEART THROB HIT PARADE

"Come back when you grow up little girl, you're still living in a paper doll world" BOBBY VEE

"Between shows there were lines of kids just waiting for pictures or autographs... And by the time you knew it, you were back on stage again" BOBBY RYDELL

"Everybody there was on cloud nine – it was an amazing time, because the electricity just floated through the air" HAL BLAINE

"It just fired Elvis up to be in front of fans again at the Comeback Special. He had a charisma where he and the audience became one thing. Not just the little girls, but also women and everybody got caught up in it" MIKE DEASY

"The Sixties were different in an isolated place. We got two television channels if the wind was blowing in the right direction. The radio stations went off at sundown. Then you picked up Chicago and heard the teenage music you really yearned for" CHARLES FRAZIER

"The Sixties are now considered a historical period, just like the Roman Empire" DAVE BARRY

"I don't regret what I did in the Sixties. I was young and took myself terribly seriously" TARIQ ALI

"I'm a child of the Sixties. I grew up with a president who was a crook, who put us into the most unpopular war in history, who had no communication with people under thirty. I had seen the Symbionese Liberation Army and the Panthers and the Diggers; I understood what they were about" JERRY HELLER

"For me, the lame part of the Sixties was the political part, the social part. The real part was the spiritual part" JERRY GARCIA

"I was born in 1952, so obviously the Sixties were important. That's when I came of age. It was also a revolutionary period, a complete break with the generation before us in terms of culture, literature, music, and in politics, of course. 1968 was an important year; I was 16, and the world became clear to me, visible, so to say" PER PETTERSON

"I grew up in the Fifties and Sixties and remember how unpleasant all kinds of food could be then" ART MALIK

"I like to think of my behavior in the Sixties as a 'learning experience'. Then again, I like to think of anything stupid I've done as a 'learning experience'. It makes me feel less stupid" P. J. O'ROURKE

"It's very hard to have lived through the Sixties and not be political" JOE DANTE

"A lot of the idealism of the Sixties was spot on, from the environmentalism to the war to the Civil Rights movement, the women's rights movement, you name it" STEVEN VAN ZANDT

"I'M A CHILD OF THE SIXTIES" IAN McSHANE

"HEY BABY WON'T YOU TAKE A CHANCE?

"For goodness sakes
I got the hippy hippy shake
Well, I got the shake
I got the hippy hippy shake"
THE SWINGING BLUE JEANS

"Work like you don't need the money. Love like you've never been hurt. Dance like nobody's watching" SATCHEL PAIGE

SAY THAT YOU'LL LET ME HAVE THIS DANCE"

CHRIS MONTEZ

"It's the latest, it's the greatest
Mashed potato, ya, ya, ya, ya
Mashed potato started long time ago
With a guy named Sloppy Joe
You'll find this dance is so cool to do
Come on baby, gonna teach it to you"
DEE DEE SHARP

"Here we go loop de loop
Here we go loop de li
Here we go loop de loop
On a saturday night"
JOHNNY THUNDER

"It's pony time, get up
Boogety, boogety, boogety shoo"
CHUBBY CHECKER

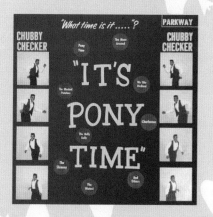

"The night we were dancin' the Strand
We fell in love as if it were planned
You saw me standin' all alone
We did the Strand
You walked me home
It was so grand
Dancin' the Strand"
MAUREEN GRAY

"AND NOW I WOULD LIKE TO QUOTE FROM ONE OF THE GREATEST WRITERS OF ALL TIME, ANONYMOUS!"

"My wife has a wonderful way to make a long story short. She interrupts"

"I always wanted to spend more time with my kids. Then one day I did"

"The summertime is when, if the girl next door comes over and asks you to light her fire, she's talking about a barbecue"

"Pacifists are people who are opposed to violence. That's why they never serve in the army, navy, marines, or get married"

"There's nothing unusual about our TV set. It has three kids in front and two installments behind"

"It's one of those hospitals where they have all kinds of code words for unpleasant things. For instance, patients never die. They just take a turn for the hearse!"

"There's a brand-new scent that's driving teenagers out of their minds. They've never experienced anything like it. It's called 'Clean'!"

"Sexual equality is creating all kinds of interesting new problems. I know a girl who's pregnant and she isn't sure it's hers"

"I always travel by bus. I have nothing against planes – but I've never heard of a bus running out of gas and falling up!"

"My teenager got a summer job. He's a short order cook in what used to be our favorite diner"

"Revolution is when it's all over quickly. Evolution is when it takes a long time. It's kinda like what happens to your sex life"

"An X-rated movie is an underdeveloped plot with an overdeveloped cast"

"A cease-fire is when trigger mortis sets in"

"Arrogance is the humility of the insecure"

"If you think education is expensive, try ignorance"

"A mistake is a lesson on its way to being learned"

"Woman was made from man's rib, which, as any butcher will tell you, isn't the best cut"

"If you want to know what it's like to be really ignored in this world – put up a stop sign in Lovers' Lane"

"Do you ever get the feeling that all you need to be a folk singer is an open mind and a closed nose?"

"Did you hear about the small-town doctor who's also the mortician? He specializes in eye, ear, nose and croak"

"It doesn't make sense, like the headline: Impotence is on the rise"

"Thanks to nuclear bombs you don't ever have to worry about waking up and hearing that war has been declared. If you wake up, it hasn't"

The Ad-Libber's Handbook: 2000 New Laughs for Speakers by Robert Orben

"TOMORROW'S SOUND, TODAY"

"We had the skirts with the slits up the side, sort of tough, sort of Spanish Harlem cool, but sweet too" RONNIE SPECTOR

"Spector kept rock'n'roll alive while Elvis was in the army" JOHN LENNON

"Spector is a good guy, but he's a nut. Ha ha ha! You know, I love him, but he's unpredictable. He's OK as long as he don't drink" IKE TURNER

"I felt obligated to change music to art, the same way that Galileo proved the Earth was round to the world and that the Sun did not stand still" PHIL SPECTOR

"Phil had thirteen hits in a row without a miss. Around 'River Deep, Mountain High' people started to want him to fail" JACK NITZCHE

"I am so thankful for the genius of Phil Spector, for his recognition of my talent to be the main voice of his Wall Of Sound" DARLENE LOVE

"What he heard in the studio – and his big motivation for mono – was that what he heard in the studio and captured on tape would always be that way. The down side was, it was hard work to get that all mixed. The up side was it was thrilling to work that way" LARRY LEVENE

"I was in The Teddy Bears and what did we get – one penny a record royalties" PHIL SPECTOR

"I was looking for a sound, a sound so strong that if the material was not the greatest, the sound would carry the record. It was a case of augmenting, augmenting. It all fitted together like a jigsaw" PHIL SPECTOR, Wall of Sound

"Techniques like distortion and echo were not new, but Phil came along and took these to make sounds that had not been used in the past. I thought it was ingenious" BARNEY KESSEL

"When 'You've Lost That Lovin' Feeling' hit, we were doing a show called 'Shindig!' and the Righteous Brothers suddenly became big business" BILL MEDLEY

Back To MONO

SPECTOR

"I think drugs were used by me as a way of suppressing my natural spirit"
MARIANNE FAITHFULL

"I loathed school. The headmistress said my clothes were too with-it"
TWINKLE

"I only wanted to be a songwriter. I never wanted to be a singer. And I never wanted to be famous"
CAROLE KING

"Sometimes I sound like gravel, and sometimes I sound like coffee and cream"
NINA SIMONE

LET'S HEAR IT FOR THE GIRLS

"I love singing. There's nothing quite like what happens between an audience and performer"
PETULA CLARK

"Years ago I learned to be totally responsible for Dionne Warwick"
DIONNE WARWICK

"On stage I make love to 25,000 different people, then I go home alone"
JANIS JOPLIN

"I wasn't aware of it at the time, but I was a big favorite with the Mafia"
BRENDA LEE

"Without Dick Clark playing "Who's Sorry Now" I wouldn't have stayed in show business"
CONNIE FRANCIS

"My parents were mad about music and that's what formed my life"
LULU

"Diamonds never leave you… men do!"
SHIRLEY BASSEY

"Anybody that'll stand up to The Cline is alright"
PATSY CLINE

"I burp like everyone else and I'm promiscuous"
DUSTY SPRINGFIELD

"Being a singer is a natural gift. It means I'm using the gift that God gave me"
ARETHA FRANKLIN

"I helped make the Sixties swing, and I'm very proud of that"
CILLA BLACK

"HAIR IS THE FIRST THING. AND TEETH THE SECOND. HAIR AND TEETH. A MAN GETS THOSE TWO THINGS HE'S GOT IT ALL"

JAMES BROWN

"The hardest thing about being James Brown is I have to live. I don't have no down time"

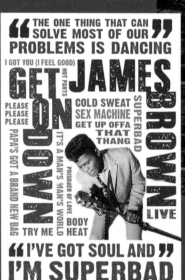

★THE★ SENSATIONAL SIXTIES

SAY IT LOUD — I'M BLACK AND I'M PROUD

James Brown

PLEASE! PLEASE! PLEASE!

THE ONE THING THAT CAN SOLVE MOST OF OUR PROBLEMS IS DANCING

I GOT YOU (I FEEL GOOD)
HOT PANTS
GET JAMES ON DOWN BROWN LIVE
COLD SWEAT
SEX MACHINE
GET UP OFFA THAT THANG
SUPERBAD
PLEASE PLEASE PLEASE
PAPA'S GOT A BRAND NEW BAG
IT'S A MAN'S MAN'S MAN'S WORLD
PRISONER OF LOVE
BODY HEAT
TRY ME

I'VE GOT SOUL AND I'M SUPERBAD

"My expectations of other people, I double them on myself"

"The one thing that can solve most of our problems is dancing"

"When I'm on stage, I'm trying to do one thing: bring people joy. Just like church does. People don't go to church to find trouble, they go there to lose it"

"I play for the kids. But it's not wild screaming that I do. I scream in the right key! It makes a difference"

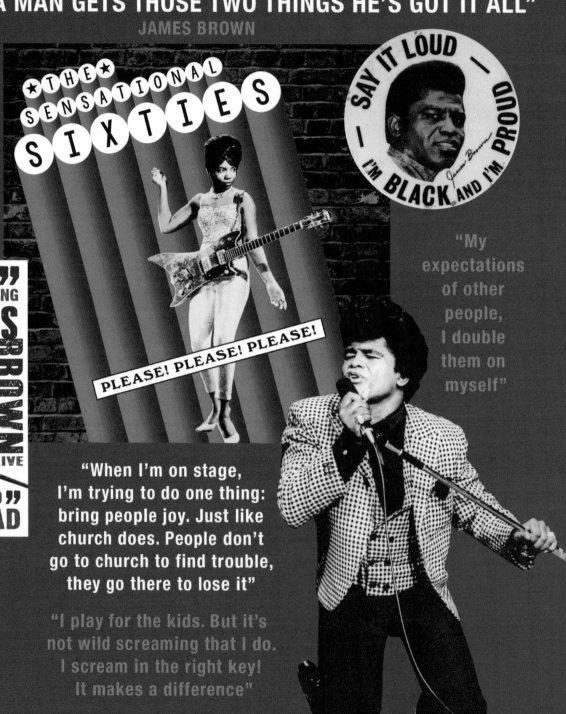

"I BELIEVE I WAS AHEAD OF MY TIME" IKE TURNER

"After I moved with my mother to St Louis, my older sister and I went to see Ike Turner, who was the hottest then. His music charged me. I was never attracted to him, but I wanted to sing with his band" TINA TURNER

"You hear me through Tina. I do it all. I do every bit of it. Every note that's played. When you saw Ike and Tina, every step came from me. All that shit came dead out of me" IKE TURNER

"PHYSICAL STRENGTH IN A WOMAN – THAT'S WHAT I AM" TINA TURNER

"Tina's said I always messed around with other women, and that's true, I won't deny it. If you want to set a trap for me, bait it with pussy – you'll get me every time" IKE TURNER

"Ike's problem was that he was a musician that always wanted to be a star; and was a star, locally, but never internationally... so he then changed the name to Ike and changed my name to Tina because if I ran away, Tina was his name. It was patented as you call it" TINA TURNER

"I always had long legs. When I was young, I used to think, 'Why do I look like a little pony?'" TINA TURNER

"MOTOWN WAS ABOUT MUSIC FOR ALL PEOPLE – WHITE AND BLACK, BLUE AND GREEN, COPS AND ROBBERS. I WAS RELUCTANT TO HAVE OUR MUSIC ALIENATE ANYONE" BERRY GORDY

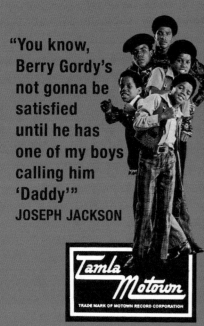

"You know, Berry Gordy's not gonna be satisfied until he has one of my boys calling him 'Daddy'"
JOSEPH JACKSON

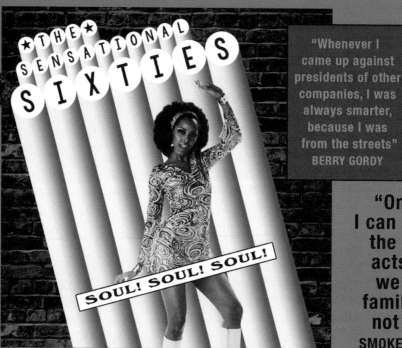

"Whenever I came up against presidents of other companies, I was always smarter, because I was from the streets"
BERRY GORDY

"One thing I can say about the Motown acts is that we were a family. That's not a myth"
SMOKEY ROBINSON

"Detroit turned out to be heaven, but it also turned out to be hell"
MARVIN GAYE

"With the Supremes I made so much money so fast all I wanted to do was buy clothes and pretty things. Now I'm comfortable with money and it's comfortable with me" DIANA ROSS

"Nobody was a better mechanic than Motown's Junior Walker, nobody"
WILSON PICKETT

"I will always dance in the street"
MARTHA REEVES

"IF EVER THERE WAS A PIECE OF MUSIC THAT DESERVED THE EPITHET 'TIMELESS', IT'S BOOKER T & THE MGs' GREEN ONIONS"
BARNEY HOSKYNS

"If you took a little of Sam Cooke and a little of Little Richard and poured it in a jar and shook it up you would get Otis Redding"
STEVE CROPPER

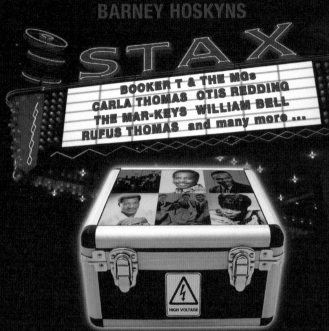

STAX

BOOKER T & THE MGs
CARLA THOMAS   OTIS REDDING
THE MAR-KEYS   WILLIAM BELL
RUFUS THOMAS and many more ...

"Bob Dylan gave me 'Just Like A Woman' to make as a record. But I just didn't feel it"
OTIS REDDING

"On 'King & Queen', Otis is all guttural, a growling bearlike alpha male, and Carla (Thomas) a sophisticated, sensual brainbox (she was studying for her English Masters at the time)"
IAN McCANN

"Walking the dog I'm just walking the dog If you don't know how to do it I'll show you how to walk the dog"
RUFUS THOMAS

"THAT'S ONE SMALL STEP FOR A MAN,

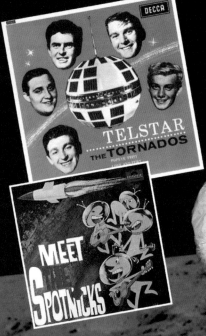

TELSTAR
THE TORNADOS

MEET SPOTNICKS

2001: a space odyssey

FIRST LUNAR LANDING OF MANKIND 1969

FRICTION POWERED
SPACE MAN

BATTERY POWERED
MOBILE SATELLITE
TRACKING STATION

IT'S Cragstan for TOYS

BATTERY OPERATED
MOON EXPLORER
#1027

"Houston, Tranquillity Base here. The Eagle has landed"

"Mystery creates wonder and wonder is the basis of man's desire to understand"
NEIL ARMSTRONG

"There's a historical milestone in the fact that our Apollo 11 landing on the Moon took place a mere 66 years after the Wright Brothers' first flight"
BUZZ ALDRIN

ONE GIANT LEAP FOR MANKIND"

NEIL ARMSTRONG

"Here men
from the
planet Earth
first set
foot upon
the Moon.
July 1969 AD.
We came in
peace for
all mankind"

NEIL ARMSTRONG

"Poyekhali!
(Let's go!)"

"If you
haven't met
God on earth,
you won't find
Him in space"
YURI GAGARIN

I'LL TRY ANYTHING ONCE

INTO THE FUTURE!

"If I've told you once, I've told you a hundred times. Do not fan the girls when they're wet! But you'll never learn, you'll be a eunuch all your life"
A FUNNY THING HAPPENED
ON THE WAY TO THE FORUM

"Martha! Damn it! I wonder what women talk about when the men are talking. I must find out sometime"
WHO'S AFRAID OF VIRGINIA WOOLF?

"Cutting off her nipples with a pair of garden shears. You call that normal? My God. Garden shears?"
REFLECTIONS IN A GOLDEN EYE

"You see, in this world there's two kinds of people, my friend: those with loaded guns and those who dig. You dig"
THE GOOD, THE BAD, AND THE UGLY

"Some days, you just can't get rid of a bomb" BATMAN

"What we've got here is failure to communicate" COOL HAND LUKE

"Don't be stupid, be a smarty, come and join the Nazi Party!"
THE PRODUCERS

"HAL, I won't argue with you anymore. Open the doors. HAL, HAL, HAL, HAL, HAL" 2001: A SPACE ODYSSEY

"The last time I made love on a ship was the Titanic. Unfortunately, we never finished"
WHAT'S UP, TIGER LILY?

"They're coming to get you, Barbra"
NIGHT OF THE LIVING DEAD

"Please sir, I want some more"
"More?!" OLIVER!

"Take your stinkin' paws off me, you damned dirty ape!"
PLANET OF THE APES

"Well, come see a fat old man sometime! Hyah!"
TRUE GRIT

"I'm Spartacus"
SPARTACUS

"If they move, kill 'em"
THE WILD BUNCH

"Think ya used enough dynamite there, Butch?"
BUTCH CASSIDY
AND THE SUNDANCE KID

"SUPERCALIFRAGILISTICEXPIALIDOCIOUS"
MARY POPPINS

HOLLYWOOD

"We rob banks" BONNIE AND CLYDE

"The Von Trapp Family don't play, they march" THE SOUND OF MUSIC

"Uh, well, sir, I – I ain't a for-real cowboy, but I'm
one hell of a stud" MIDNIGHT COWBOY

"Well, you're pretty sure of yourself, ain't ya, Virgil. Virgil,
that's a funny name for a nigger boy to come from Philadelphia.
What do they call you up there?"
"They call me Mister Tibbs" IN THE HEAT OF THE NIGHT

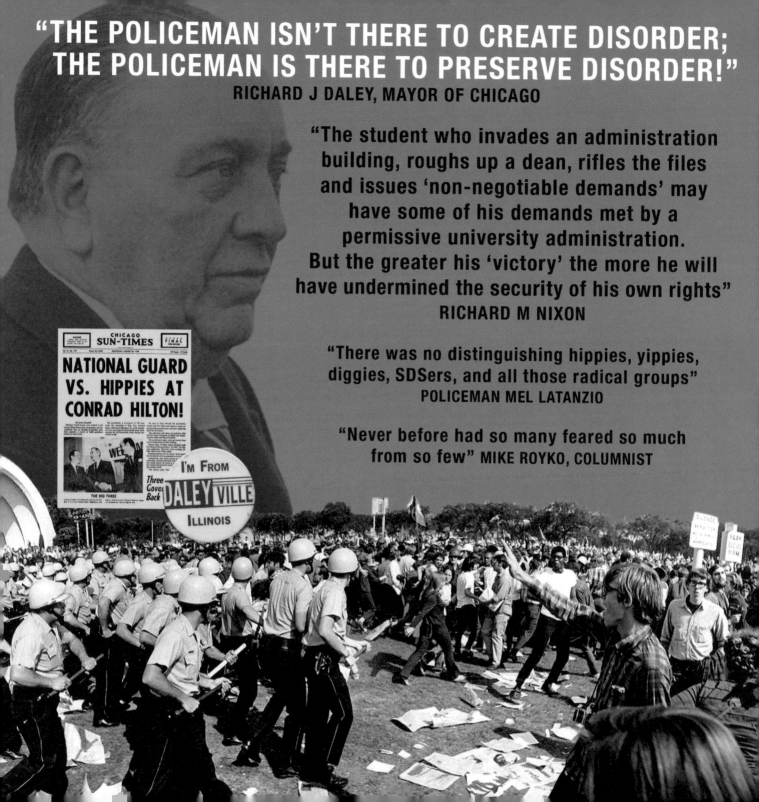

"THE POLICEMAN ISN'T THERE TO CREATE DISORDER;
THE POLICEMAN IS THERE TO PRESERVE DISORDER!"
RICHARD J DALEY, MAYOR OF CHICAGO

"The student who invades an administration building, roughs up a dean, rifles the files and issues 'non-negotiable demands' may have some of his demands met by a permissive university administration.
But the greater his 'victory' the more he will have undermined the security of his own rights"
RICHARD M NIXON

"There was no distinguishing hippies, yippies, diggies, SDSers, and all those radical groups"
POLICEMAN MEL LATANZIO

"Never before had so many feared so much from so few" MIKE ROYKO, COLUMNIST

CHICAGO SUN-TIMES FINAL

NATIONAL GUARD VS. HIPPIES AT CONRAD HILTON!

I'M FROM
Three
Gover
Back DALEYVILLE
ILLINOIS

"The Black Panthers are the greatest threat to the internal security of the country" J. EDGAR HOOVER

"Revolution is about the need to re-evolve political, economic and social justice and power back into the hands of the people, preferably through legislation and policies that make human sense. That's what revolution is about. Revolution is not about shootouts" BOBBY SEALE

"The Black Panther Party was not a gang. They grew out of a young black intelligentsia on college campuses"

"If they had not murdered Malcom X, there probably never would have been a Black Panther Party"

"You don't fight racism with racism, the best way to fight racism is with solidarity"

"We were like heroes, to stand there and observe the police, and the police were scared to move upon us"

BOBBY SEALE

"Now, then, in order to understand white supremacy we must dismiss the fallacious notion that white people can give everybody their freedom" STOKELY CARMICHAEL

"I expected to die. At no time before the trial did I expect to escape with my life. Yet being executed in the gas chamber did not necessarily mean defeat. It could be one more step to bring the community to a higher level of consciousness"

"You can jail a Revolutionary, but you can't jail the revolution"

"We have two evils to fight, capitalism and racism. We must destroy both racism and capitalism"

"Sometimes if you want to get rid of the gun, you have to pick the gun up"

"My fear was not of death itself, but a death without meaning"

HUEY NEWTON

"We're not in Wonderland anymore Alice"

CHARLES MANSON

"Everything that's realistic has some sort of
ugliness in it. Even a flower is ugly when it
wilts, a bird when it seeks its prey, the ocean
when it becomes violent" SHARON TATE

"It's weird, I always had the premonition that
Sharon belonged to me for just a little while"

ROMAN POLANSKI

"Believe me, if I started murdering people,
there'd be none of you left" CHARLES MANSON

"This could destroy Roman. Marriage
vows mean nothing to him but few men
have adored a woman as much as
he adored Sharon" LAURENCE HARVEY

"I was at a party three weeks prior
to the murders at Roman Polanski
and Sharon Tate's house"

NANCY SINATRA

"Sanity is a small box,
insanity is everything"

CHARLES MANSON

"DID I KILL ANYONE?"

CHARLES MANSON

FINAL SUNDAY NEWS **20¢**
NEW YORK'S PICTURE NEWSPAPER

ACTRESS AND 4
SLAIN IN RITUAL

Sharon
Tate
Among
Victims

"The Rolling Stones are violence. Their music penetrates the raw nerve endings of their listeners and finds its way into the groove marked 'release of frustration'" JON LANDAU

"Michelle Phillips of the Mamas And The Papas came, bearing tales of how the Angels were fighting with civilians, women, and each other, bouncing full cans of beer off people's heads" **STANLEY BOOTH**

"I was talking to a couple of the Angels when the tent flap wobbled and one of them whacked it with a billiard cue – there was probably some kid's head behind it. When it came time for us to go on, the Angels made a line for us to pass through. I felt very worried as we walked to the stage" **CHARLIE WATT**

"We both saw the commotion when the guy got stabbed. We saw the whole thing, and my heart skipped a beat" **BILL WYMAN**

"I thought the scene in San Francisco was supposed to be so groovy. It was terrible. If Jesus had been there he would have been crucified" **MICK JAGGER**

"I was distressed to find the boxing kangaroo had been axed. I had also missed Mick wrestling a live tiger" **KEITH ALTHAM**

"The Rolling Stones' 1969 US Tour was a remarkable tour at a remarkable time. Some say Altamont – the free concert tacked on to the end – ended the Sixties" ETHAN A RUSSELL

"Good morning! What we have in mind is

"The New York state freeway's closed, man, far out!" ARLO GUTHRIE

"Woodstock – I didn't see anybody play, except when I was standing backstage waiting to go on, because it was so muddy. And the weather was so horrible, you literally couldn't get there except by helicopter"
GRACE SLICK

"Woodstock was both a peaceful protest and a global celebration"
RICHIE HAVENS

"I played Woodstock in '69, and it really changed my life. Without a doubt, it was the single event that really changed the way I felt about music. Up to that point, I hadn't really thought of myself as a more serious musician, and I didn't really have that much interest in pop music"
EDGAR WINTER

breakfast in bed for 400,000"
WAVY GRAVY

"Woodstock had a tremendous impact on American artistic life" PJ O'ROURKE

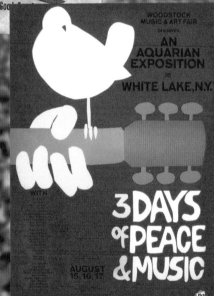

Woodstock Music and Art Fair

FRIDAY
August 15, 1969
10 A. M.
$8.00
Good For One Admission Only
47976 NO REFUNDS

Woodstock Music and Art Fair

SATURDAY
August 16, 1969
10 A. M.
$8.00
Good For One Admission Only
47976 NO REFUNDS

Woodstock Music and Art Fair

SUNDAY
August 17, 1969
10 A. M.
$8.00
Good

WOODSTOCK
MUSIC & ART FAIR
presents
AN
AQUARIAN
EXPOSITION
in
WHITE LAKE, N.Y.

3 DAYS of PEACE & MUSIC

AUGUST
15, 16, 17

"The Woodstock dove on the iconic poster is really a catbird. And it was originally perched on a flute" SHAWN AMOS

"SOMEBODY HAS TO DO SOMETHING AND IT'S JUST

"I'm a lumberjack and I'm OK
I sleep all night and I work all day
I cut down trees, I wear high heels
Suspendies and a bra
I wish I'd been a girlie, just like my dear Papa"
MONTY PYTHON

"That's probably what's going to happen: some brilliant kid will come along and be popular. I can see a lone artist with a lot of tapes and electrical ... like an extension of the Moog synthesizer — a keyboard with the complexity and richness of a whole orchestra, y'know? There's somebody out there, working in a basement, just inventing a whole new musical form" JIM MORRISON, ROLLING STONE INTERVIEW 1969

"In 1969, I gave up women and alcohol – it was the worst 20 minutes of my life"
GEORGE BEST

"I've been the male equivalent of the dumb blonde for a few years, and I was beginning to despair of people accepting me for my music. It may be fine for a male model to be told that he's a great-looking guy, but that doesn't help a singer much, especially now that the pretty-boy personality cult seems to be on the way out" DAVID BOWIE

"My guardian angel does all the writing; I'm sure it's not me" MARC BOLAN

"I realized what Led Zeppelin was about around the end of our first U.S. tour. We started off not even on the bill in Denver, and by the time we got to New York we were second to Iron Butterfly, and they didn't want to go on!" ROBERT PLANT

"If you're the Beatles in the Sixties, you just get carried away – you forget what it is you wanted to do. You're starting to do Sgt. Pepper. Some people think it's a genius album, but I think it's a mishmash of rubbish, kind of like Satanic Majesties – 'Oh, if you can make a load of shit, so can we'"
KEITH RICHARDS

"They credited us with the birth of that sort of heavy metal thing. Well, if that's the case, there should be an immediate abortion" GINGER BAKER, CREAM

"Here it is again, San Quentin, just for you
San Quentin, you've been livin' hell to me.
You've guarded me since nineteen sixty three
I've seen 'em come and go and I've seen 'em die
And long ago I stopped askin' why"
JOHNNY CASH

"I may make you feel but I can't make you think ... your sperm's in the gutter, you love's in the sink" JETHRO TULL

"It's an example of non-violence. Imagine if the American army stayed in bed for a week, and the Vietnamese army ... or President Nixon or Chairman Mao. Imagine if the whole world stayed in bed. There'd be peace for a week, and they might get to feel what it's like" JOHN LENNON

"The Monkees are like the mafia. You're in for life. Nobody gets out" DAVY JONES

"Without deviation from the norm, progress is not possible" FRANK ZAPPA

"Arnold Layne had a strange hobby" SYD BARRETT

"INCREDIBLY PATHETIC THAT IT HAS TO BE US"
GERRY GARCIA

"All you really need is love, but a little candy now and then doesn't hurt" CHARLES SCHULZ

"I used to live on one candy bar a day: it cost a nickel. I always remember the candy bar was called Payday. That was my payday. And that candy bar tasted so good, at night I would take one bite, and it was so beautiful"
CHARLES BUKOWSKI

"A candy cane allows me to walk with a fat stomach"
ANTHONY T. HINCKS

"Since all culture is a kind of con game, the most dangerous candy you can hand out is one which causes people to start questioning the rules of the game"
TERENCE McKENNA

"Candy is dandy but liquor is quicker"
UNKNOWN

Brach's Easter Candy Sale!

"Sweets for my sweet, sugar for my honey
Your first sweet kiss thrilled me so
Sweets for my sweet, sugar for my honey
I'll never ever let you go"
THE SEARCHERS

"My boy lollipop
You make my heart go giddy up
You are as sweet as candy
You're my sugar dandy"
MILLIE SMALL

"New rule: someone must x-ray my stomach to see if the Peeps I ate on Easter are still there, intact and completely undigested. And I'm not talking about this past Easter. I'm talking about the last time I celebrated Easter, in 1962" BILL MAHER

"FREEDOM IS SOMETHING THAT DIES UNLESS IT'S USED"
HUNTER S THOMPSON

"I'll tell you what freedom is to me; no fear.
I mean really, no fear!" NINA SIMONE

"Conformity is the jailer of freedom and the enemy of growth"
JOHN F KENNEDY

"A hero is someone who understands the responsibility that comes with his freedom"
BOB DYLAN

"Tame birds sing freedom. Wild birds fly"
JOHN LENNON

"Freedom is not enough"
LYNDON B JOHNSON

"May 24, 1961: Twenty-seven Freedom Riders, headed for New Orleans, were arrested as soon as they arrived in the bus station in Jackson, Mississippi. Many of the riders were sentenced to two months inside Mississippi's worst prison, Parchman" JERRY MITCHELL, THE CLARION-LEDGER

"ON THE OTHER SIDE OF FEAR LIES FREEDOM" UNKNOWN

"Let us not seek to satisfy our thirst for freedom by drinking from the cup of bitterness and hatred"
MARTIN LUTHER KING

"AFTER YOU GET YOUR FREEDOM, YOUR ENEMY WILL RESPECT YOU"
MALCOLM X

A selection of images featured in this book plus other designs are available on T-shirts, posters, phone cases, cushions, mugs, notebooks, postcards, etc, www.redbubble.com/people/tigerdaver

A selection of albums from PlayDigital
to stream or download at www.amazon.co.uk

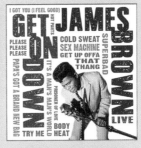

"The '60s are gone, dope will never be as cheap, sex never as free, and the rock'n'roll never as great" ABBIE HOFFMAN

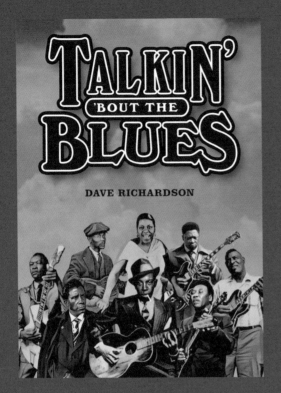
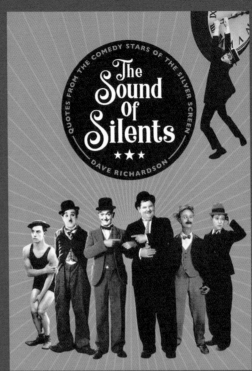

Printed in Great Britain
by Amazon